HAL LEONARD GUITAR METHOD

ACOUSTIC GUITAR

ISBN   978-0-634-06452-4

WITHDRAWN

HAL•LEONARD® CORPORATION
7777 W. BLUEMOUND RD. P.O. BOX 13819 MILWAUKEE, WI 53213

Visit Hal Leonard Online at **www.halleonard.com**

INTRODUCTION

Welcome to the Hal Leonard Acoustic Guitar Method. This book supplements the concepts and techniques taught in the Hal Leonard Guitar Method, concentrating specifically on the subject of acoustic guitar. Though the book begins with the basics, there is plenty of material for the more experienced player as well. Elementary examples are included to demonstrate certain techniques, followed by excerpts from real songs. The Beatles, the Goo Goo Dolls, Robert Johnson, and many more will demonstrate how the many concepts covered in this book can be applied in real-world musical situations. What better way to learn the essentials of acoustic guitar playing than from the pros themselves? Let's get on with it.

TABLATURE & CHORD GRIDS

Guitar players have long used a number system called *tablature*, or "tab" for short, as a means of guitar notation. Tablature consists of six horizontal lines, each representing a string on the guitar. The top line represent the high E string, second line the B string, third line the G string, and so on. A number on the line indicates the fret number at which you play the note.

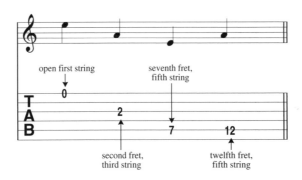

open first string · seventh fret, fifth string · second fret, third string · twelfth fret, fifth string

Some examples make use of *chord grids*. In case you're unfamiliar with these, here's a look at how they're read. The six vertical lines represent the six strings on the guitar, from low to high (left to right).

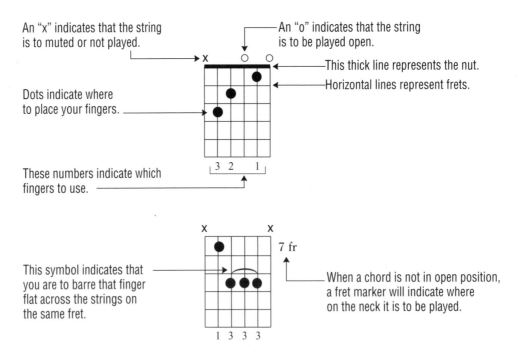

An "x" indicates that the string is to muted or not played.

An "o" indicates that the string is to be played open.

This thick line represents the nut.

Horizontal lines represent frets.

Dots indicate where to place your fingers.

These numbers indicate which fingers to use.

This symbol indicates that you are to barre that finger flat across the strings on the same fret.

When a chord is not in open position, a fret marker will indicate where on the neck it is to be played.

ABOUT THE AUDIO 🔊

The CD includes demonstrations of many examples in this book. A full-length song, with which you can jam along and practice your newly acquired skills, appears at the end of each chapter. The corresponding track number for each song or example is listed below the audio icon.

CHOOSING AN ACOUSTIC GUITAR

When purchasing your first acoustic, you're likely to be overwhelmed by the endless choices available today. Virtually every aspect of the guitar will affect its tone, including the type of wood, presence of a cutaway, type of bracing, and even the finish. The intent of this section is to provide some guidelines that will hopefully make the task of choosing the right equipment a bit easier.

Guitars, like most musical instruments, are very personal objects. Players often develop a strong attachment to their instrument when they find one that feels right to them. No two player's hands or arms are exactly alike, and the feel of a guitar is equally important as the sound or look. You may have your heart set on buying the guitar used by your favorite player. If, however, when you try that guitar out for yourself and it just doesn't feel right to you, you'd be better off continuing your search rather than forcing the instrument onto yourself. Remember, you're going to be spending (hopefully) a lot of time on the instrument, and you don't need it fighting you. With the myriad of options available, you're sure to find the sound, look, and feel that you prefer if you're just willing to shop around a bit.

SIZE AND TYPE

Within the realm of the acoustic guitar, there are many different types available. Here we'll look at a few of the most common variations and their characteristics.

Dreadnought

The dreadnought is a large instrument with a full sound and ample bass, commonly used to accompany vocals. This is by far the most common type of acoustic and is probably what most non-guitarists picture in their head when they think "acoustic guitar." Sometimes called a "Western" guitar, dreadnoughts are manufactured from many different types of wood and range in price from under a hundred to several thousand dollars (as is the case with all of the types mentioned here). The Martin D-28 is one of the most popular of all dreadnought models.

Folk or Parlor Style

This guitar is much smaller in size and usually slightly quieter than a dreadnought. Due to the reduced size, the frequency response of these guitars is usually more balanced, resulting in an even, pronounced sound favored by fingerstyle players in particular. The Larrivee Parlor guitar is a popular instrument in this category.

Jumbo

As the name implies, the jumbo is the largest style of acoustic guitar and, as you might expect, produces a big, booming sound. These guitars usually have prominent bass frequencies. The sound is similar to that of a dreadnought, but often times the midrange is slightly more pronounced in a jumbo. Their timbre usually sits well within a mix of many different instruments, making them a common choice for pop artists. The Gibson SJ-200 is one such instrument commonly employed.

12-String

The 12-string acoustic is widely available in all of the above-mentioned sizes, except for the folk style. The top two courses (pair of strings) are unisons, while the bottom four are octaves, giving this instrument a shimmering sound that can liven up the most pedestrian of strumming patterns. (Think "Hotel California" by the Eagles.) Some common 12-strings include the Guild F212 XL and the Gibson J-185 12.

Martin D-28

Larrivee Parlor guitar

Gibson SJ-200

Gibson J-185 12

OTHER CONCERNS

Aside from the size and type, there are a few other variations to consider when choosing your instrument.

Cutaway

Virtually all of the above-mentioned types are available in a cutaway model. While the effect on the sound caused by the cutaway is the subject of some debate, a well-made model shouldn't suffer any serious tonal loss. The sound will be affected, though, however subtle the difference may be. The obvious advantage lies in the access to the higher frets. If you don't plan on reaching the stratosphere region of your acoustic fretboard, though, a cutaway model isn't necessary.

Electric Acoustic

In certain instances, practicality will be the determining factor when choosing your instrument. For instance, if you're going to be playing acoustic within a live band situation, you may want to look into an electric acoustic. These are available in all of the previously mentioned formats (including cutatway models) and have become arguably as popular as standard acoustics in many circles. These instruments feature an installed pickup that allows you to plug them into an amplifier as you would an electric guitar. Different types of pickups are used, including piezo (installed under the saddle), magnetic soundhole types (wedged into the soundhole), and contact pickups (mounted to the inside or outside of the soundboard). Generally speaking, it's safe to say that the plugged-in sound of your acoustic isn't going to accurately replicate the unplugged sound. The more expensive types of pickups do a better job, but it's still not quite the same. However, they will make the acoustic guitar loud enough to compete with the other instruments in the band.

Many electric acoustic models feature on-board controls, such as volume and EQ, which will allow you to somewhat shape the sound to fit your needs. EQ settings can range from a simple "tone" control to a full-blown 3-band (bass, mid, and treble).

Amplification

As for amplification, there are now several amps on the market made specifically for acoustic guitars. Many of these also include a channel for vocals as well, with an XLR mic input and separate level and EQ controls. These are oftentimes a perfect choice for the singer/songwriter looking to play smaller venues where just a slight amount of amplification is needed. Alternatively, direct boxes are commonly employed, along with various processors (EQs, compressors, effects boxes, etc.), to plug an acoustic directly into a channel on the PA mixer. This method will also allow you to further shape the sound of the guitar, as the mixer will usually possess some type of EQ as well.

If you simply can't get used to the sound of an electric acoustic, there is another possibility for amplification: using a microphone. Generally speaking, this will produce the tone of the guitar more faithfully than any pickup can, but there are several things to consider. The first is freedom of movement. When playing with a microphone, you're going to be stuck in front of it and not permitted to move more than six or eight inches. Because of this, microphones are usually used when sitting down. Another concern is feedback. Though a unidirectional mic will help with this issue, sometimes it's still necessary to enlist the help of an EQ or some type of "feedback eliminator" device to identify and eliminate the offending frequencies. Recently, some internally (or externally) mounted microphones have become available, combining the practicality of a pickup with the sound of a mic. Though these types of systems will usually run in the higher range, if you're not willing to compromise your sound for anything, this may be your best route.

Fernandez Cutaway

Fender Electric Acoustic

Fender Acoustic Amp

CONSTRUCTION AND WOOD TYPE

Probably the most significant aspect in the tone of an acoustic guitar is the type of wood used. The sound, look, and durability are all factors when choosing woods. There are several commonly used woods today, and each one colors the sound in its own way. It's also not uncommon for a guitar to use one type of wood for the back and sides and another type for the top (soundboard).

Following is a list of some of the most commonly used woods and some of their characteristics:

Soundboard

Sitka spruce: Consistent, uniform grain and good overall tonal response.

Englemann spruce: A light wood in both color and weight, with a slightly louder and more "open" tone than Sitka.

Koa: Extremely beautiful grain with a predominant treble response and slightly less volume than spruce.

Western red cedar: An extremely light wood with great clarity of sound and good volume.

Genuine mahogany: A less projective wood with more emphasis on midrange

Back and Sides

East Indian rosewood: An extremely resonant wood usually red, brown, and dark purple in color producing a warm bass response, especially on larger guitars.

Brazilian rosewood: Nearly extinct, therefore very expensive and limited in availability. The color ranges from dark brown to violet and commonly contains attractive streaks in the grain, while the tonal response is nicely balanced.

Morado: Finer in texture but closely resembles East Indian rosewood in appearance and tonal qualities.

Koa: A golden brown wood with dark streaks containing slightly less bass response than rosewood and slightly less treble response than maple, but a balanced tone nonetheless.

European flamed maple: A hard, reflective wood containing an attractive rippled pattern through the grain producing a loud, powerful sound.

All of this information is fine and good, but it's a bit subjective. Different players have ears for different guitars, and until you get out and play one, it's hard to make a decision. If you're not able to get your hands on many guitars and demo them, try to find out what guitars are making sounds that you like on record. For instance, Eric Clapton uses a Martin guitar with a Sitka spruce top and an East Indian rosewood back and sides. Bob Dylan recorded *Bringing It All Back Home* with a Gibson Nick Lucas Special. This guitar featured Brazilian rosewood for the back and sides and red Adirondak spruce for the top. The Beatles often made use of the Gibson J-160E in the early days, which featured solid Sitka spruce on the top and mahogany for the back and sides. James Taylor makes use of a custom made Olson guitar combining a cedar top with East Indian rosewood back and sides.

Guild D55

Seagull M6

Taylor 915 CE

CHAPTER 1: STRUMMING

Although presumably the easiest of guitar techniques, it's amazing how many guitarists neglect basic chord strumming. A strong command of strumming is probably the most important skill you can develop in acoustic guitar playing, especially if you intend to accompany yourself or someone else singing.

Learning chord shapes is only half the battle. A solid right-hand technique is a must if you want to be able to make people move! In this chapter, we'll work our way from basic to more intermediate strumming patterns, all the while observing how the techniques are applied in real songs.

Before we get started, let's take a look at some of the most common chords you're likely to encounter. When playing through these, keep the following in mind:

- Make sure all the notes in the chord are ringing out clearly. Try plucking each string individually; If one note sounds muted or muffled, chances are a finger is touching the string unintentionally or you're fretting too lightly.

- An "x" on a chord grid indicates that a string should not be sounding at all. In the case of a C chord, for example, you don't want the low E (sixth) string to ring. There are a few ways to accomplish this: 1) Allow the tip of your third finger to touch the sixth string, deadening it. 2) Bring your left-hand thumb over the top of the neck to lightly touch the sixth string. 3) Begin your strum from the fifth string.

   I highly recommend one of the deadening methods (options 1 or 2), as the third method requires an impractical amount of precision when actively strumming. If you get into the habit of deadening the strings that you're not play- ing, you can strum away and not have to worry about avoiding certain strings. This may require a slight adjustment to your typical fretting technique, but nothing drastic.

- Don't get discouraged! If you're just beginning, your fingers are going to get a little sore at first. As you play more, you'll build up calluses on your fingertips.

- Fingernails are not your friends! Keeping them trimmed will make playing chords much easier.

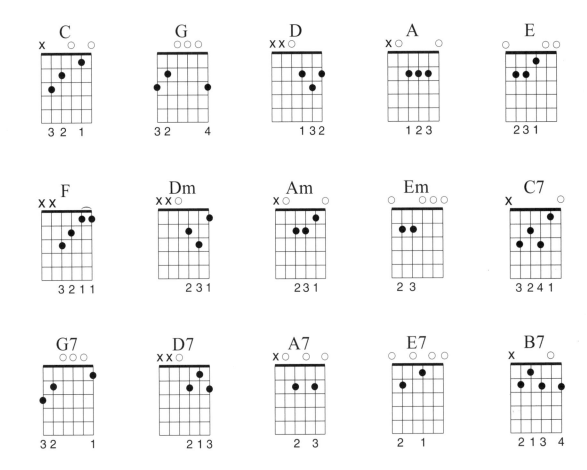

DOWNSTROKES & UPSTROKES

One of the most important factors in developing a solid strum technique is consistency. Your strumming hand needs to be a solid and steady timekeeper, and this is made much more difficult if you're having to think about how to strum each particular rhythm. If, however, you're consistently employing some basic strumming principles, you'll soon find that you can often leave your right hand on autopilot. The guidelines within this chapter should leave you adequately prepared to tackle almost any strumming pattern you encounter without giving it a second thought.

Try these first few examples. Pay special attention to the strumming indications: ⊓ = downstroke, and V = upstroke. Notice that downstrokes are used for all the downbeats (1, 2, 3, 4), while upstrokes handle all the upbeats (the "and"s). This simple concept is very important to master, as it's fundamental to many more advanced strumming patterns. It may help to count out loud along with the examples at first.

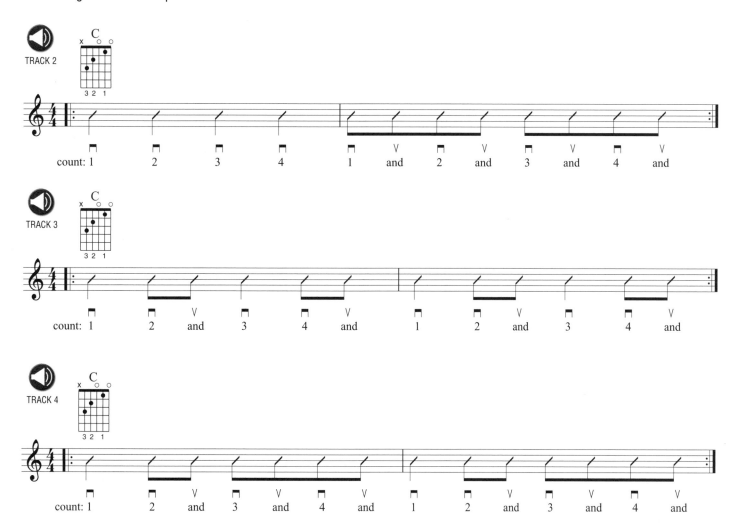

In this next example, which consists of straight eighth notes, you may want to start experimenting with placing the accent (or stress) on different beats throughout the pattern. This simply entails strumming harder when you want to accent a beat. Try accenting beats 2 and 4 of each measure, for example, and notice how the pattern comes to life.

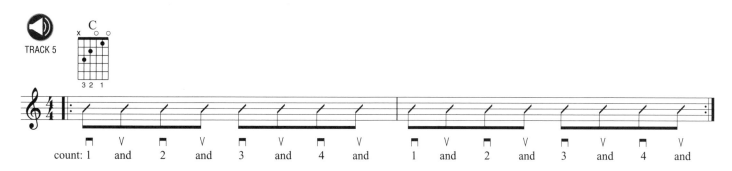

MOVING FROM CHORD TO CHORD

When learning to transition between two chords, start out very slowly. In this example we're moving from C to G while maintaining the same strumming pattern. What you *don't* want to do is chug along on the C chord in tempo, then pause, and then pick the tempo back up for the G chord. Instead, start slow at the beginning and increase the tempo only when you're able to change chords without dropping a beat.

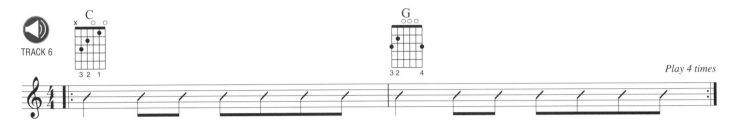

Our next example uses four chords: C, Am, Dm, and G7. This example illustrates an important technical point to consider when changing chords: *common tones.* This means that two chords share one or more notes. This can often be exploited on the guitar. Notice the similarity between the C chord and the Am chord. The only thing that needs to happen is the movement of your third finger from the C note on the fifth string (fret 3) to the A note on the third string (fret 2). Your first and second fingers don't need to move at all. This lends a great continuity to chord changes. Even if only one finger remains stationary when changing chords, it makes for much smoother rhythm playing. This same thing happens again when changing from the Dm to G7. The first finger can remain on the F note on the first string.

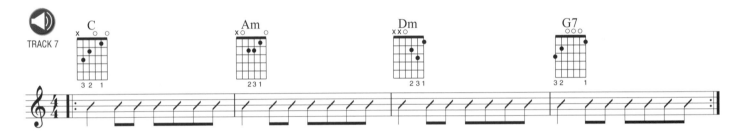

Next, we see another invaluable chord-changing tool: the *open-string strum.* When you're not able to leave a common finger in place during a chord change, you'll usually need a little more time to lift and replant all your fingers. To avoid breaking the rhythm, you can simply strum the top few strings with an upstroke while you change chords. If you listen closely to these next two examples, you'll hear that the last eighth note in each measure is actually the open top few strings. In most moderate-to-quick tempos, the effect will be negligible to the ear.

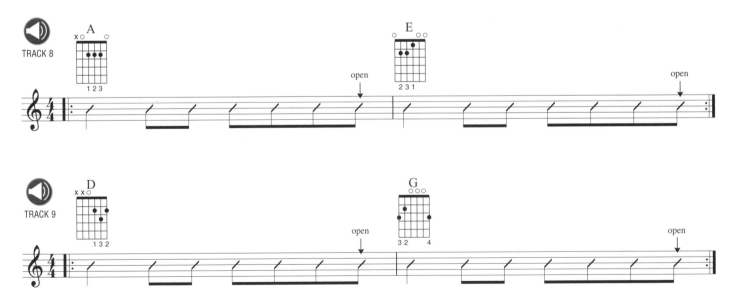

The last chord-changing concept we'll cover is the *muted strum.* While the open-string strum is commonly employed with open chords, the muted strum is often used when playing barre chords. (If you're unfamiliar with *barre chords*, you may as well learn them now because they're essential to know. They require you to lay a finger—across several strings on the same fret.) The following example makes use of E-form barre chords built off the sixth string. When moving between barre chords, the fret-hand pressure is temporarily released, creating a muted, percussive sound when strumming. Again, this effect is usually not noticeable at moderate tempos. If barre chords are new to you, don't expect to nail these right away; it may take a while to build up the strength needed to play them cleanly. NOTE: Some players prefer to fret the sixth string by wrapping their thumb around the top of the neck, barring only the top few strings with their first finger. Experiment with both methods and see which one suits you.

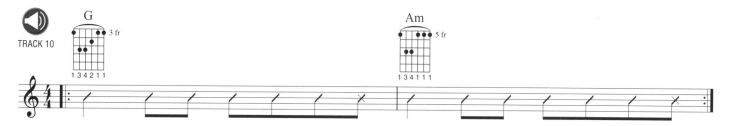

Here we see the A-form chords built off the fifth string. On the major form, the third finger is usually used to barre across strings 4, 3, and 2. String 1 may be muted by the third finger as it begins to slightly bend backward.

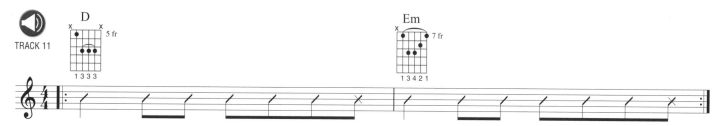

Syncopation

To *syncopate* means to place a stress on a weak beat. Syncopation plays a major role in many strumming patterns, so it's essential to gain a strong command of the technique. In the following example, we're accenting the "and" of beat 2. Notice that the strumming pattern still pairs downstrokes with downbeats and upstrokes with upbeats. This requires a "ghost stroke" on beat 3. By ghost stroke, I mean your right hand continues in a downstroke motion, but your pick does not contact the strings. If this feels awkward to you, realize that you have already been employing ghost upstrokes; they just weren't apparent. In the first example of the chapter, for instance, you strummed all downstrokes in a quarter-note rhythm. In order to do this, you had to bring your pick back up during the "and" of each beat (the upbeat) without contacting the strings. This essentially reverses that; you're bringing your pick down without contacting the strings.

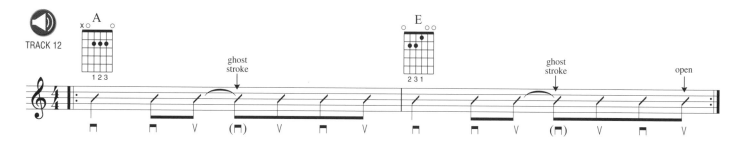

Here we're accenting the "and" of beat 4. This is another common syncopated rhythm you're bound to encounter.

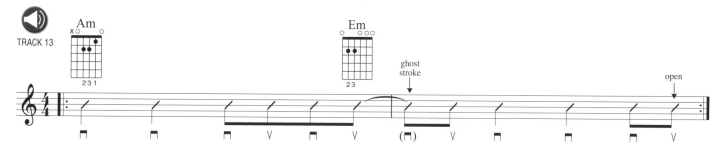

Now let's take a look at some classic strumming riffs that make use of all the elements we've looked at so far.

MAGGIE MAY

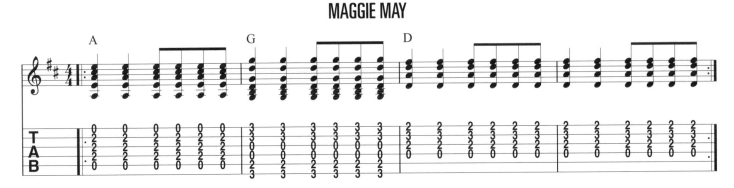

BAND ON THE RUN

TRACK 14

SHOW ME THE WAY

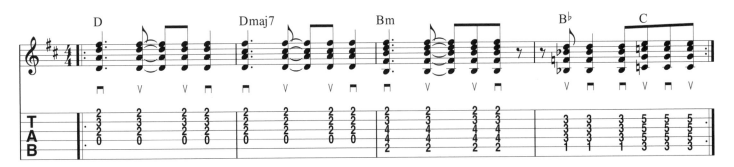

LEAVING ON A JET PLANE

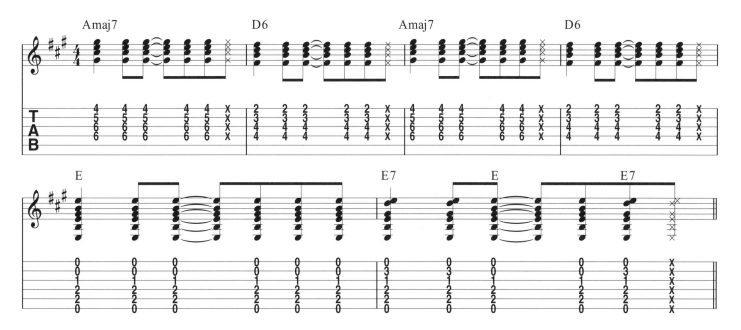

Words and Music by John Denver
Copyright © 1967 Cherry Lane Music Publishing Company, Inc. (ASCAP) and DreamWorks Songs (ASCAP)
Rights for DreamWorks Songs Administered by Cherry Lane Music Publishing Company, Inc.
International Copyright Secured   All Rights Reserved

SIXTEENTH NOTES

So far, all of our examples have consisted of eighth-note strumming rhythms. But what about strum patterns that make use of sixteenth notes? Which ones are upstrokes and which ones are downstrokes? It may help to think of simply *double-timing* an eighth-note pattern. In other words, downstrokes will be used for all the eighth notes, and upstrokes will handle the sixteenth notes in between. Try the example below, paying close attention to the strumming indications. It may help to count along.

TRACK 15

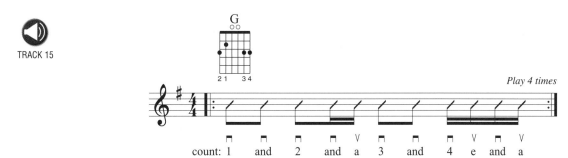

Just as eighth notes can be syncopated, so can sixteenth notes, as this example demonstrates. Remember that the right hand should be moving consistently down and up, ghosting strokes when needed to provide the syncopation.

TRACK 16

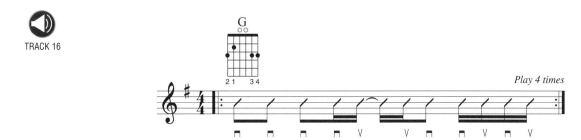

11

Now, let's take a look at a few songs that make use of sixteenth-note strum patterns.

BEHIND BLUE EYES

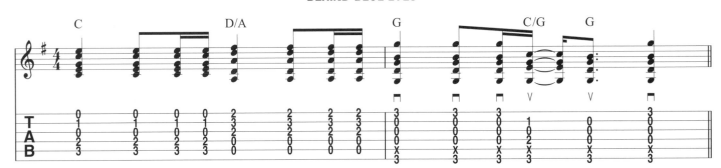

LET HER CRY

CLOSER TO FINE

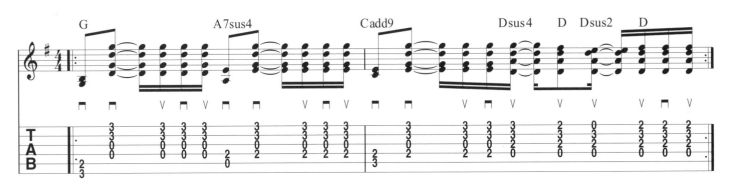

JAM SESSION

Now it's time to put what you've learned to use with a full-length jam track. Duncan Sheik had a standout hit in 1996 with the acoustic-driven "Barely Breathing." In this tune, you're going to encounter a little bit of everything, including syncopated rhythms, "dead" notes (or muted strums), and common tones and fingerings. Notice how the strumming pattern is altered slightly to delineate the different sections. You may want to practice different patterns (verse, chorus, etc.) separately before attempting to put them all together.

Here are a few more things to keep in mind: Notice that, other than the A7 chord, your third finger can remain on the D note throughout the entire intro and verse progression. On the A7 chord, you simply need to slide it down a half step to C♯. Also, the only chord in the entire song that strays from open position is the Fmaj9/C in the chorus, immediately following the Am chord. To make this shift as smooth as possible, be sure to notice that fingers 1, 2, and 3 remain in the same shape for both chords—you'll just need to shift them down one set of strings for the Fmaj9/C chord.

BARELY BREATHING

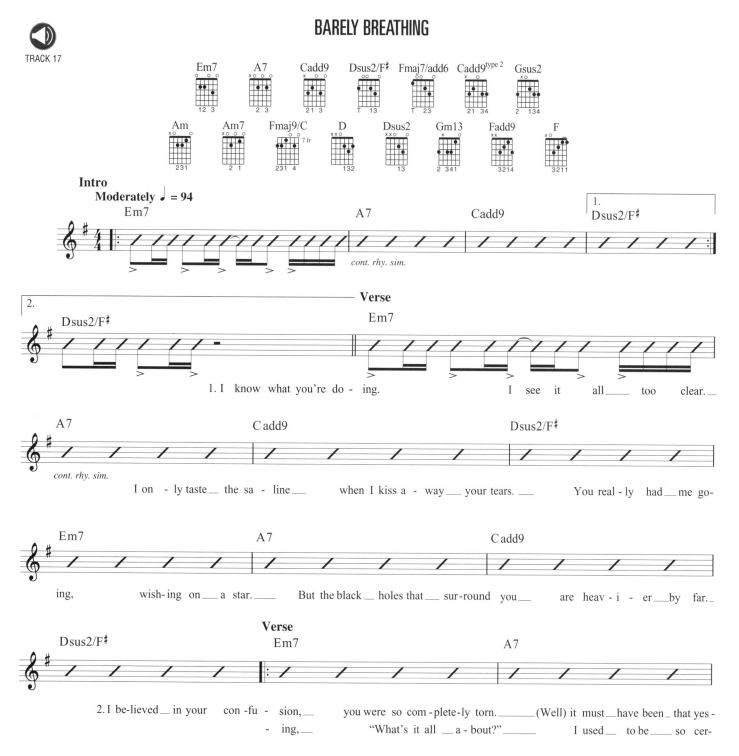

Words and Music by Duncan Sheik
Copyright © 1996 by Careers-BMG Music Publishing, Inc., Duncan Sheik Songs and Happ-Dog Music
All Rights Administered by Careers-BMG Music Publishing, Inc.
International Copyright Secured All Rights Reserved

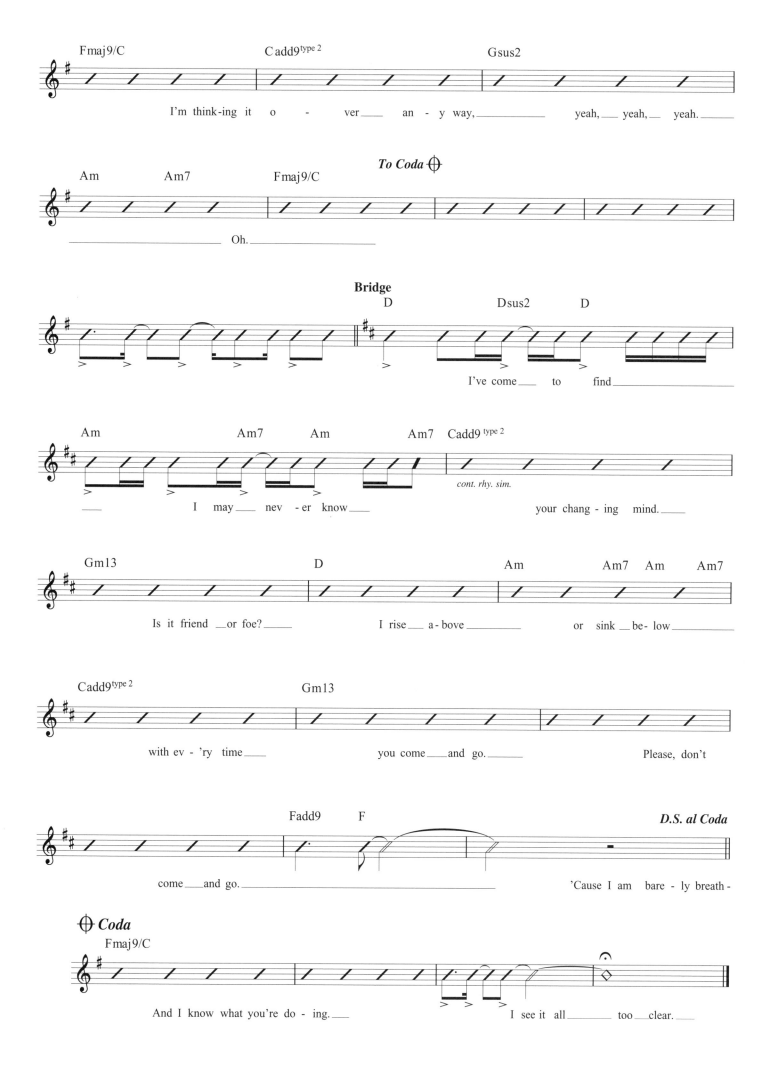

Fmaj9/C   Cadd9 type 2   Gsus2

I'm think-ing it o - ver____ an - y way,_____ yeah,___ yeah,___ yeah.____

To Coda ⊕

Am   Am7   Fmaj9/C

_____ Oh._____

Bridge
D   Dsus2 D

I've come___ to find_____

Am   Am7 Am   Am7 Cadd9 type 2

cont. rhy. sim.

___ I may___ nev - er know____   your chang - ing mind.___

Gm13   D   Am Am7 Am Am7

Is it friend ___ or foe? ___   I rise ___ a - bove _____ or sink ___ be - low_____

Cadd9 type 2   Gm13

with ev - 'ry time_____   you come___ and go. _____   Please, don't

Fadd9 F   ***D.S. al Coda***

come___ and go. ___   'Cause I am bare - ly breath -

⊕ ***Coda***

Fmaj9/C

And I know what you're do - ing. ___   I see it all_____ too ___ clear. ___

CHAPTER 2: FINGERPICKING

Now that you've gotten a good handle on strumming, let's throw the pick aside for a bit and work with our bare hands. Though fingerpicking is most closely associated with folk and rockabilly styles, we'll learn in this chapter how it can be applied to many more.

When guitarists begin to feel at home with the pick, they often shy away from learning to play fingerstyle because it can feel like "starting from scratch." This sentiment is certainly justified; it is in a way like starting over again. However, only one hand needs to learn something new. Also, it should be noted that many players prefer the use of a thumbpick when playing fingerstyle. Whether you choose to try one or not (they can be quite handy in moving between fingerstyle and strumming quickly), all the exercises in this chapter will still apply just the same.

TRAVIS PICKING

Perhaps the most common fingerstyle technique is *Travis picking*. Popularized by country legend Merle Travis, the technique usually involves the thumb alternating between two bass notes while the fingers "fill in the holes" on the treble side.

This first example demonstrates a basic Travis picking pattern that should help you get a feel for the technique. Note the fingering indications for the right hand: T = thumb, 1 = first finger, 2 = second finger, etc.

TRACK 18

Here we're moving between C and G chords. Notice the difference in the thumb pattern: we're rocking back and forth between strings 6 and 4 on the G chord. It should be noted that the "and" of beat 2 is often slightly accented in Travis picking patterns such as these, providing a gentle syncopation that helps create a sense of momentum. Also notice that we're not playing string 5 during the G chord at all. This means, for all practical purposes, that we don't have to fret that string. Of course, there's nothing wrong with fretting that string if you so choose; the point is that you have the option.

TRACK 19

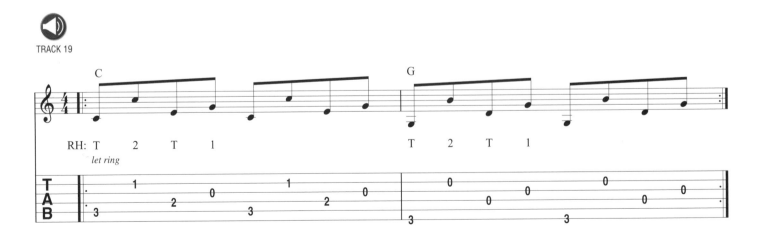

Now that you've got the basics down, let's take a look at some common variations. In example A, we're simply striking the first two notes on beat 1 at the same time, creating a quarter note instead of two eighths. In example B, the right-hand thumb is 5th every other time for the root. Example C omits the first treble note altogether, be- Example D elaborates on C, making use of the third finger to create an interesting pat- shift, which is another option when accessing higher strings. Example F elaborates on

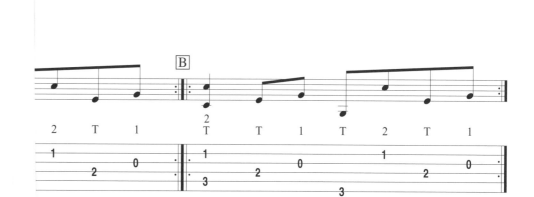

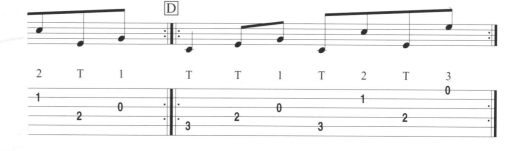

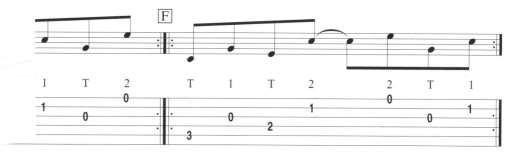

Keep in mind that these variations are often combined freely in actual musical applications. Let's take a look at a few classic Travis picking examples.

YOU WERE MEANT FOR ME

TRACK 21

*slight vibrato

Words and Music by Jewel Kilcher and Steve Poltz

ARPEGGIATION

Another common fingerstyle approach, especially on ballads, is to arpeggiate chords in a rolling fashion. This often involves striking a bass note with your thumb on beat 1 and allowing your first, second, and third fingers to finish the chord. Let's take a look at some basic examples.

This first simply arpeggiates through C and G chords in ascending fashion. Notice that although the thumb shifts positions, the right-hand fingers remains on the same group of strings. One thing to consider on a riff such as this is how to maintain a smooth transition between chords. In this example, it will help to sustain the C note (on the B string) right up until you strike the low G note on beat 3. This will assure there won't be an unwanted gap of silence.

TRACK 22

Next we see a way to maintain an even greater sense of continuity when changing chords. We've voiced the chords in such a way that a common tone (the high G) is allowed to ring throughout, creating a full, resonant sound. When working through a new progression, it's often possible to find these common tones between chords. This is a good habit to get into, as it can make the difference between a mediocre guitar part and one that really sings.

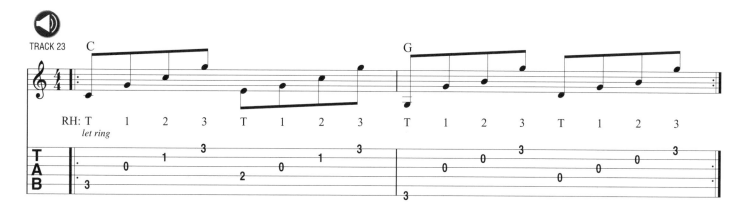

Here's a common fingerpicking pattern in 3/4 applied to a I–vi–V progression in C. Notice again the common tone (open E string). As far as fingering, here's another trick. Instead of fretting the A minor chord as you normally would (fingers 2, 3, and 1), try using fingers 2 and 1 only, for the A and C notes, respectively. Remember, since you're not playing string 4, you don't need to fret it. This way, your third finger will be free to fret the low G note at the beginning of measure 3.

TRACK 24

As our next two examples demonstrate, you can also combine arpeggiation with simultaneously struck notes. This can help to break up the monotony and provide additional interest for the listener.

TRACK 25

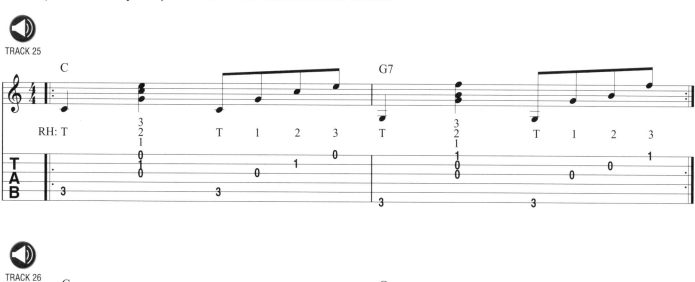

TRACK 26

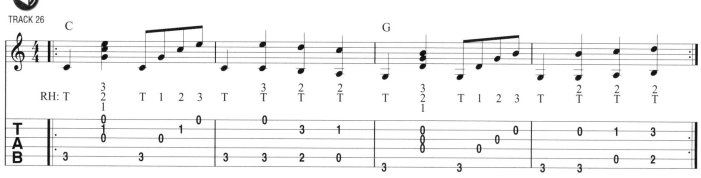

Let's take a look at a few songs that make use of arpeggiation.

TIME IN A BOTTLE

ANNIE'S SONG

STRONG ENOUGH

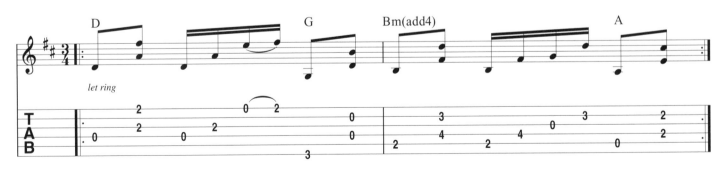

TRACK 27

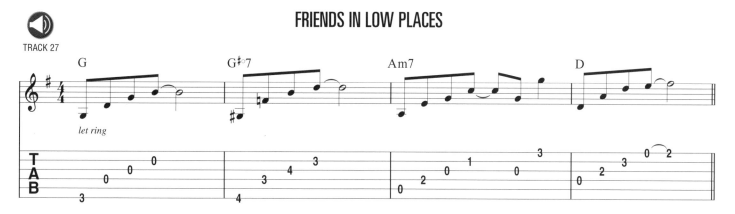

BLOCK CHORD STYLE

Aside from Travis picking and arpeggiation, there's still other fingerstyle approaches. One of the most common is the *block-chord* style (where several notes are struck at the same time). Let's take a closer look at this approach.

Here's a basic example of the block-chord style. In this example, the right-hand thumb handles the bass notes, and the fingers (1, 2, and 3) pluck all the treble notes.

TRACK 28

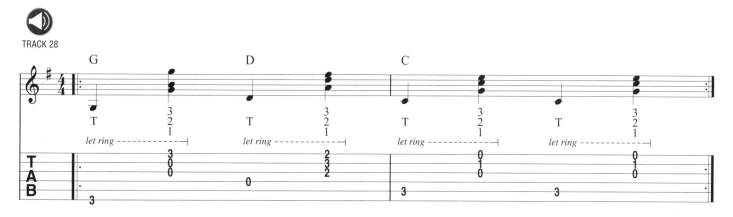

With a little syncopation, some make-do percussive sounds, and variation, we can turn the previous example into a nice little riff. The "X" notes on beats 2 and 4 are accomplished by simply "planting" your right-hand fingers on the appropriate strings with much more force than normal. On beat 2 of measure 1, for example, you would bring your right hand down in preparation for the following D chord, with your thumb ready to strike the fourth string and your fingers on the three treble strings. But you would do this with a quick, forceful motion so that the strings slap against the frets and cause the desired percussive "smack."

TRACK 29

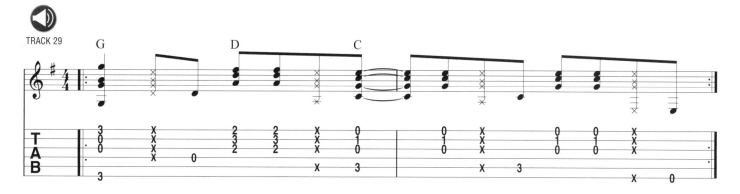

Let's take a look at a few songs that make use of the block-chord style.

YESTERDAY

TRACK 30

MORE THAN WORDS

TRACK 31

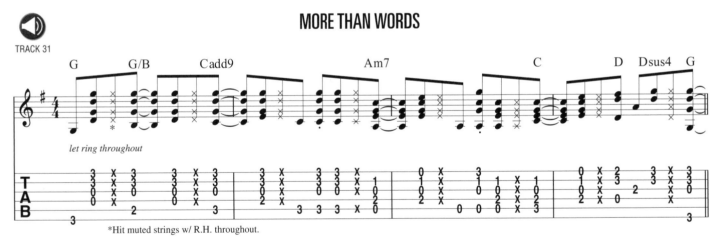

*Hit muted strings w/ R.H. throughout.

JAM SESSION

Now it's time for the jam track. "Dust in the Wind" by Kansas is perhaps one of the most popular Travis picking riffs of all time, so it's a good one to know all the way through. You can initiate campfire sing-a-longs for years to come by whipping out this timeless tune. One of the most interesting things about the intro to this song is the effect that's achieved by cycling three different melody notes in a continuous "three-over-four" fashion.

You'll get a bit of practice on most facets of Travis picking here, including the use of your right-hand third finger (in the second measure of each verse), shifting string groups, and the occasional hammer-on or pull-off embellishment. Notice the effective use of the open B string in the bridge, allowing access to the eerie, extended harmonies throughout the section.

DUST IN THE WIND

TRACK 32

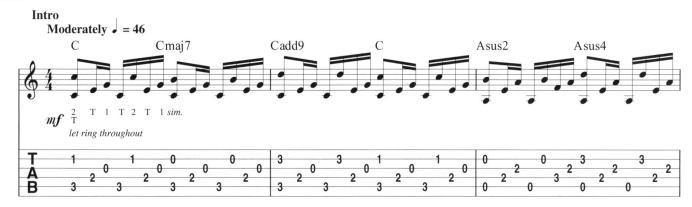

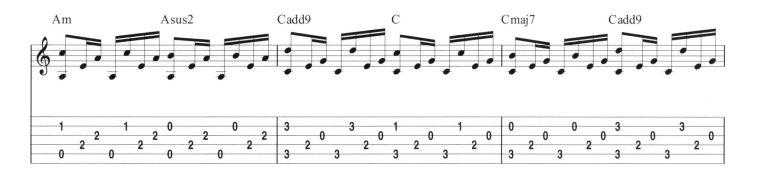

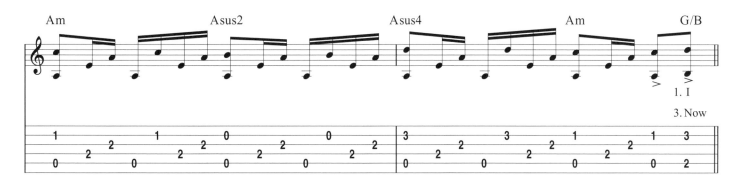

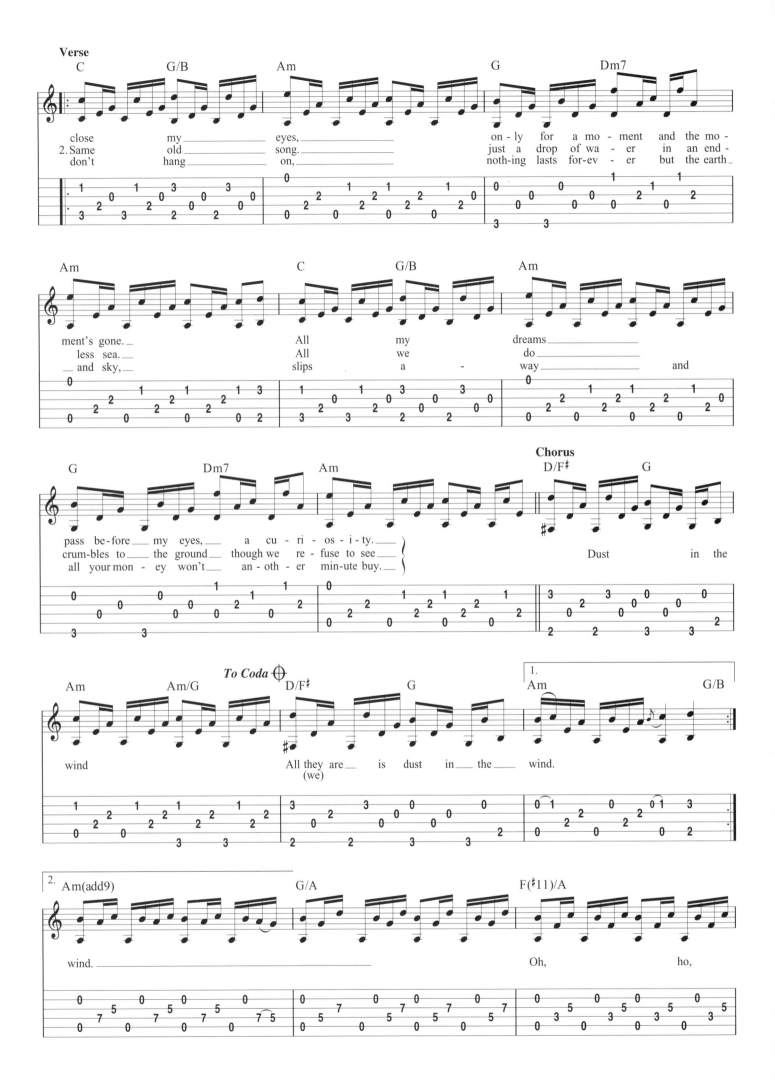

Instrumental Bridge

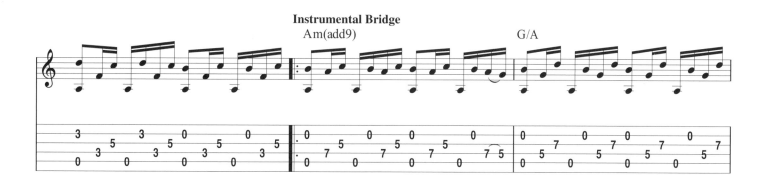

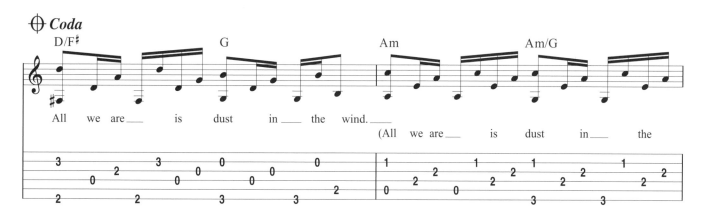

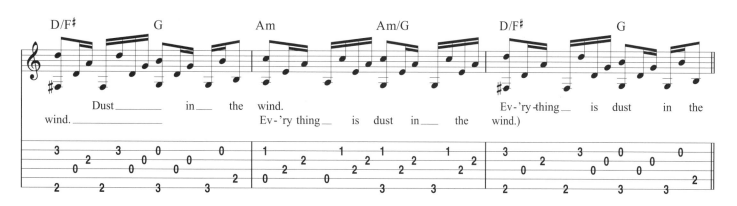

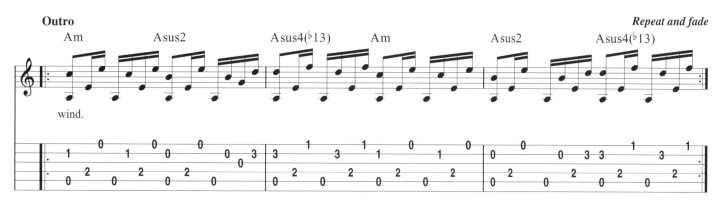

CHAPTER 3: USING A CAPO

Since the acoustic guitar is such a popular instrument for accompanying singers—i.e., yourself or another vocalist—it seems only fitting to address the issue of using a capo. This is not to say that non-singing guitarists don't have a need for them—far from it! Using a capo is in essence no different than retuning your entire guitar. Here are just a few instances when a capo can come in handy:

- **Avoiding the use of barre chords.** This is a big one, because let's face it—barre chords are just no fun. With a capo, you can often find a way to play the same chords without having to barre at all.

- **Adjusting the key of a song to fit vocal range.** If you've ever tried singing a song that was just out of your reach, you can easily slap a capo on and transpose it to a suitable key.

- **Creating an alternate or complementary guitar part.** Players often use capos when overdubbing in the studio in order to access certain voicings that aren't otherwise possible. Bands with two guitarists also employ them to avoid playing the same chord shapes, therefore creating a fuller sound.

WHAT IS A CAPO?

For those of you who aren't sure what a capo is, let's explain how it works. A capo is a device that clamps onto the neck of a guitar, barring across the strings at whichever fret you choose. In essence, it becomes a moveable nut, allowing you to raise the pitches of all the open strings evenly without having to retune the guitar. There are a few different types of capos available, with the most popular being the "quick-change" type. A "poor man's" capo can even be fashioned from a rubber band and a pen or pencil if you're flat broke! Hopefully you won't have to resort to this, however, as you can usually purchase a perfectly decent capo for around $10 or so.

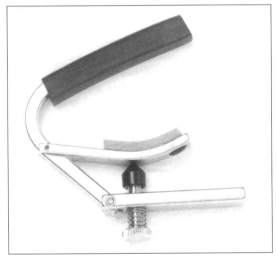

Shubb "Original" Capo

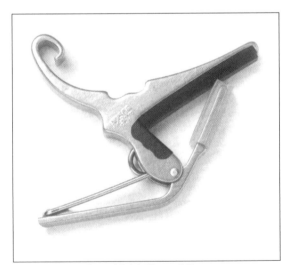

Kyser "Quick Change" Capo

So how exactly do you use a capo? Let's look at an example of each of the three instances above.

AVOIDING BARRE CHORDS

Let's say the keyboardist in your band writes a new song in B♭. He tells you he wants to have an acoustic guitar strumming the chords while he plays melodically. The chords are E♭, B♭, Cm, and Gm. Well, the capoless guitarist may say "Yuck! All barre chords! Hello, finger cramps." The crafty guitarist, however, will say, "No problem! Let me just slap a capo on fret 3 and I'll be ready to go." Let's examine this. First let's look at how you might be forced to play these chords without a capo.

TRACK 33

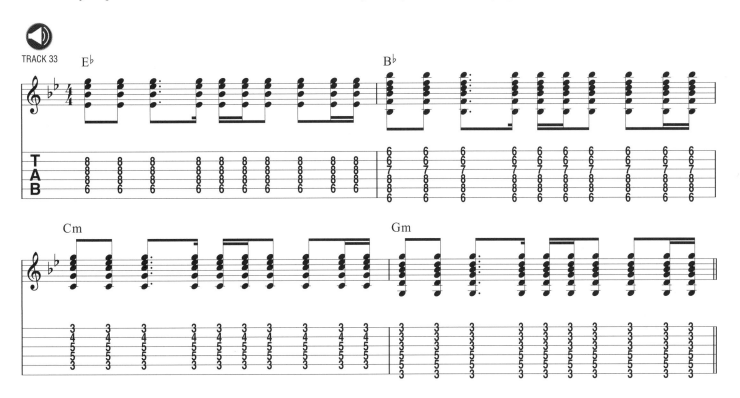

Now take a look at how easy this progression can be played with a capo on fret 3. Voila! No more barre chords!

TRACK 34

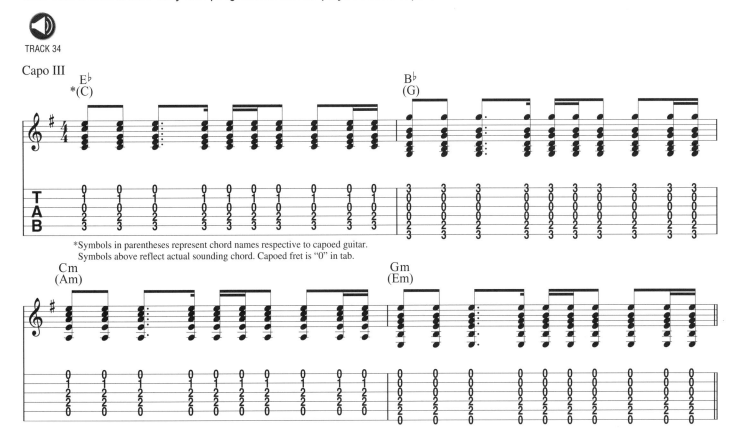

*Symbols in parentheses represent chord names respective to capoed guitar.
Symbols above reflect actual sounding chord. Capoed fret is "0" in tab.

ADJUSTING THE KEY FOR A BETTER VOCAL RANGE

OK, so you've spent a lot of time learning to play your favorite outlaw country song in the key of E. It's based around the I, IV, and V chords (E, A7, and B7). You've even learned the little chordal embellishments, and it sounds great. Now you're ready to sing along. It's all going great and then, whoa! You try your best to hit the low notes, but it ends up sounding more like a frog's croak. You have to transpose the song. You decide you need to bring it up a minor 3rd (to G) to be comfortable. After playing the song with G, C7, and D7 shapes, you notice it just doesn't sound the same as it did in E. What to do? Simply slap a capo on the third fret, and you're able to play it the way you learned it with the E, A7, and B7 shapes. See the example below.

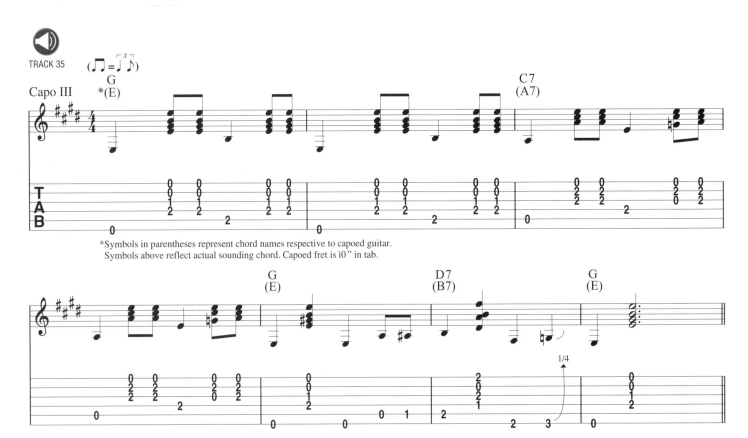

*Symbols in parentheses represent chord names respective to capoed guitar.
Symbols above reflect actual sounding chord. Capoed fret is ì0" in tab.

ALTERNATE GUITAR PART

This scenario is encountered all to often with new bands. Guitarists that often don't know any better just ending up playing the same thing. While it's not uncommon for players to double-track a guitar part in the studio to achieve a bigger sound, this is often not necessary when playing live. A song is often times better served by two complementary parts rather than a doubled one. Below we see a riff in A consisting of I, ♭VII, IV, and ♭VI chords (A, G, D, and F). Player 1 is playing big, open chords in root position. Player 2 joins in with the same thing, and it sounds great for the intro and first verse.

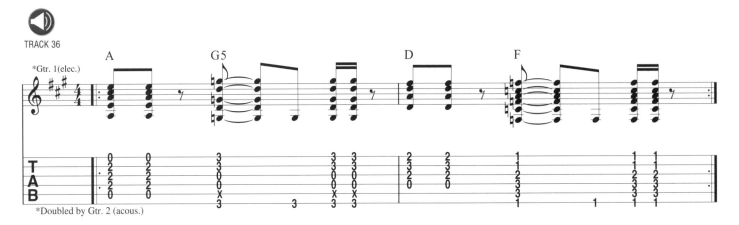

*Doubled by Gtr. 2 (acous.)

The second verse rolls around, and the singer (player 1) says, "It seems like something else should come in there. We need to maintain the interest of the listener." Since the band is a four-piece consisting of two guitars, bass, and drums, and the singer doesn't want to play anything too complicated while he's singing, the responsibility falls on player 2. Rising to the challenge, he slaps a capo on fret 5 and comes up with a decorative part that fills in the holes perfectly. And he's still able to play unison chords with player 1 for the beginning of the song. They even discover that they prefer the sound of the capoed chords doubling the electric. Of course, the song goes to #1, the band sells 5 million copies of their album, and they each become rich and famous—all because player 2 learned how to make the most out of the capo!

TRACK 37

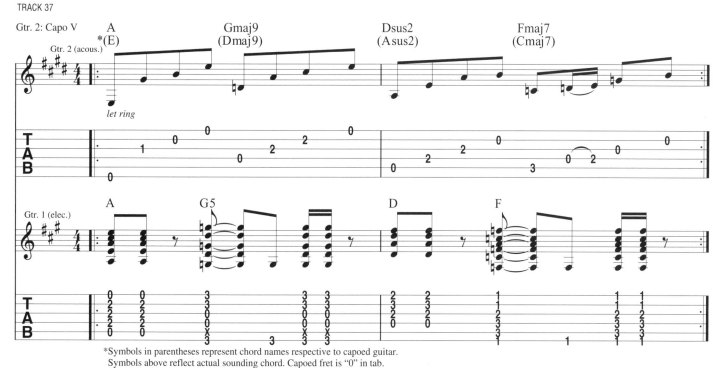

*Symbols in parentheses represent chord names respective to capoed guitar.
Symbols above reflect actual sounding chord. Capoed fret is "0" in tab.

Let's take a look at some classic capoed riffs; these will all fit into one of the three above-mentioned categories. Picking indications are included when needed to make sure you're still strumming correctly. Remember your ghost strokes!

LANDSLIDE

TRACK 38

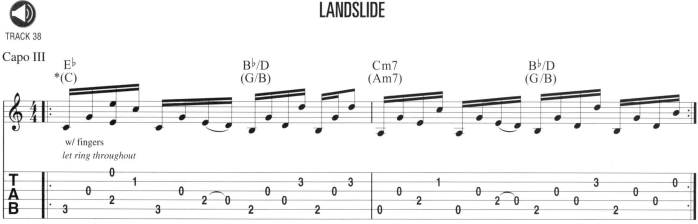

*Symbols in parentheses represent chord names respective to capoed guitar.
Symbols above reflect actual sounding chord. Capoed fret is "0" in tab.

Words and Music by Stevie Nicks
Copyright © 1975 Welsh Witch Music
Copyright Renewed
All Rights Administered by Sony/ATV Music Publishing, 8 Music Square West, Nashville, TN 37203
International Copyright Secured   All Rights Reserved

NORWEGIAN WOOD
(THIS BIRD HAS FLOWN)

*Symbols in parentheses represent chord names respective to capoed guitar.
Symbols above reflect actual sounding chord. Capoed fret is "0" in tab.

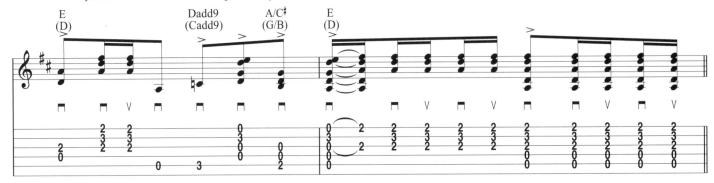

YOU'VE GOT A FRIEND

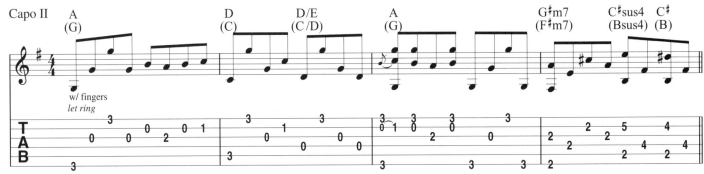

*Symbols in parentheses represent chord names respective to capoed guitar.
Symbols above reflect actual sounding chord. Capoed fret is "0" in tab.

TRACK 39

SMALL TOWN

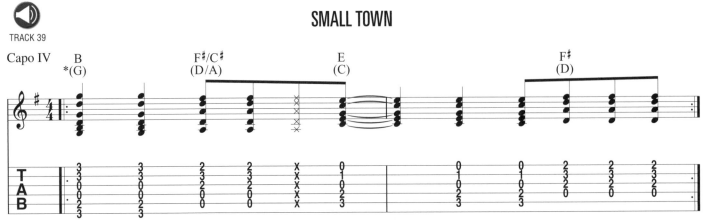

*Symbols in parentheses represent chord names respective to capoed guitar.
Symbols above reflect actual sounding chord. Capoed fret is "0" in tab.

JAM SESSION

OK, time for the jam track. George Harrison's "Here Comes the Sun," one of his most enduring Beatles contributions, features an unforgettable capo riff (see next page). Playing out of D, G, and A7 shapes, the capo at fret 7 causes this tune to sound in the key of A.

It's not as easy as George makes it sound to pick out the melody on the top two strings while strumming the rest of the chord at the same time. Since we haven't looked specifically at this type of strumming yet, let's try a few exercises first to get an idea of how it works. The main thing to keep in mind with this type of playing is to not get bogged down in details. The melody note (which is on top usually) is the most important thing. Whether or not you get all of the other notes exactly as written isn't important. Try these two examples, concentrating on bringing out the melody while maintaining a solid rhythmic feel. Notice that downbeats are still paired with downstrokes.

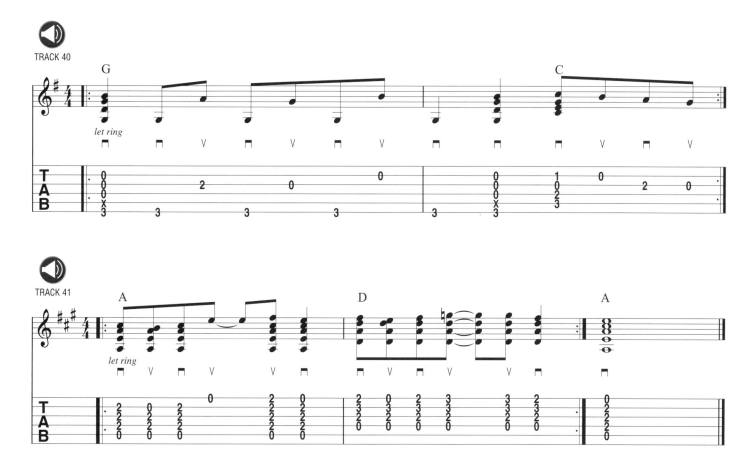

In this next example, we encounter an arpeggio figure in measure 2 similar to the one you'll find in "Here Comes the Sun." For this figure, you may find it easier to stray from alternate picking (alternating down- and upstrokes). I've included another picking indication that you may want to try. An important thing to mention about this style is that you should always be holding the chord shape while you're ornamenting with melody notes if possible. Here in measure 1, for example, you should be holding the entire E chord throughout the measure even though you're not playing the whole chord; the high F♯ note is accessed with the pinky.

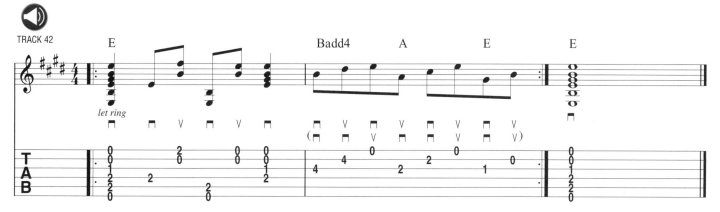

Watch out for the time signature changes in "Here Comes the Sun." You may have to listen and follow along with the audio to hear how this section plays out. Take it away!

TRACK 43

HERE COMES THE SUN

CHAPTER 4: ALTERNATE TUNINGS

Technically, an alternate tuning is created when one or more strings of the guitar are tuned to notes that differ from standard tuning (E–A–D–G–B–E). One of the most immediate benefits of an alternate tuning is the fresh perspective that it brings. If a player has never experimented with anything other than standard tuning, he or she is likely to be pleasantly surprised by the opportunities for new sounds that alternate tunings can afford. For all practical purposes, playing in an alternate tuning is many times similar to starting over on the instrument; the magic that existed with the first strumming of a G chord is awakened once more, and the player is no longer bound by familiar chords or patterns. Alternate tunings also allow the guitarist to play voicings that would be impossible in standard tuning. For this reason, they are commonly employed in studio situations, when you can spend (literally) all day getting one chord to shimmer like gold. Simply put, alternate tunings can provide a great vehicle with which to get out of a rut—a situation all too familiar to many guitarists.

It's beyond the scope of this chapter to fully explore alternate tunings, as there are no limits to the number of possible tunings. I felt compelled to include it though, as they are much more often employed in the world of the acoustic guitar. The great bluesmen of the thirties and forties made extensive use of numerous tunings, as have solo fingerstyle virtuosos such as Michael Hedges and Leo Kottke. Though there has been a recent growth in the popularity of alternate tunings in the rock guitar world, it still seems that the acoustic guitar sees most of the action. Let's examine a few of the most common alternate tunings and see what they have to offer.

OPEN G

From the bluesmen of the Delta to the Rolling Stones, open G tuning (low to high, D–G–D–G–B–D) has seen lots of action over the years. Not only does it allow you to play a chord (G major) with absolutely no fretting, it also facilitates the easy one-finger moveable barre chord. Here's how to access open G tuning from standard tuning:

1. Tune your sixth string down one whole step to match the pitch of your open D string.
2. Tune your fifth string down one whole step to match the pitch of your open G string.
3. Now tune your first string down one whole step to match the pitch of your open D string. That's it—you're in open G.

Let's take a look at some fresh-sounding chord shapes in this tuning's home key of G. Notice how the standard I, IV, and V chords sound fresh and alive again in this tuning.

TRACK 44

Open G tuning:
(low to high) D–G–D–G–B–D

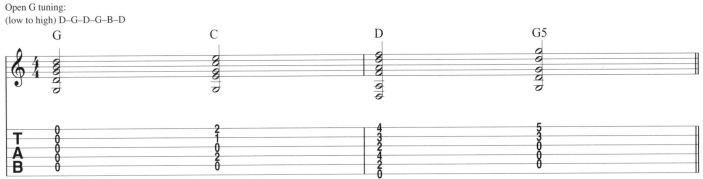

Here we're just moving the same shape up the neck while allowing strings 5 and 1 to drone open. Listen to the full-sounding chords that result.

TRACK 45

Open G tuning:
(low to high) D–G–D–G–B–D

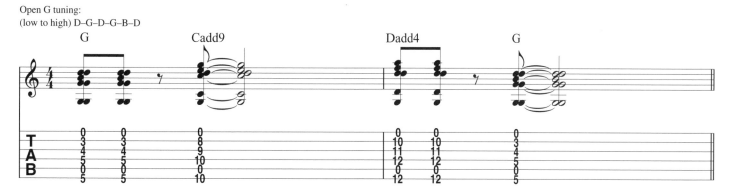

Here are several voicings each for I, IV, and V chords. Try strumming or fingerpicking them in different combinations and see what you come up with.

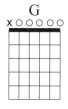
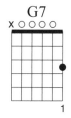
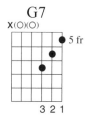
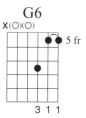

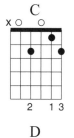
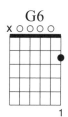
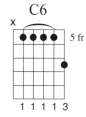
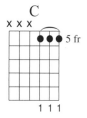
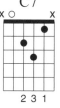

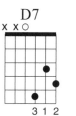

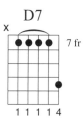

Now let's take a look at some great riffs from the pros that make use of open G.

PINK HOUSES

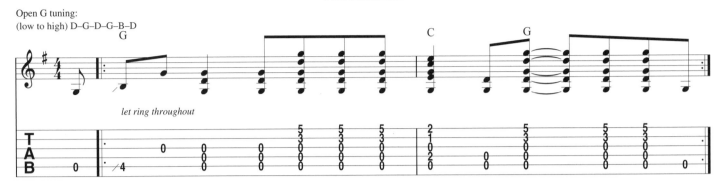

CROSS ROAD BLUES
(CROSSROADS)

DROP D

Another common alternate tuning is Drop D (low to high, D–A–D–G–B–E). This allows you to access octaves on strings 6 and 4 but keeps the rest of the guitar as you're used to it. In the realm of the acoustic guitar, Drop D is often exploited in the solo guitar genre, as it allows the thumb to drone on the open D strings while playing chords and melodies on top. The only thing you need to do in order to reach drop D from standard tuning is lower your sixth string down a whole step to match your open D string. (If you're still in open G tuning, just bring your fifth and first strings back up a whole step, and you're there.)

OK, now try this Travis picking example and see how the octave D strings can be exploited in this tuning. Notice that we're using the same open D shape for each chord, just moving it up the fretboard. For the last chord, strum all six strings with your thumb.

TRACK 46

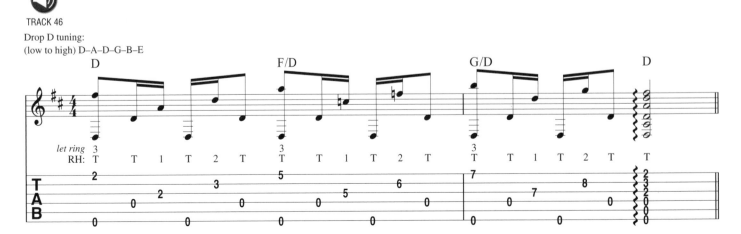

Here's another example, this time embellished with a few hammer-ons. This also features a right-hand thumb shift to strings 5 and 4 for the A chord in measure 3.

TRACK 47

Drop D tuning:
(low to high) D–A–D–G–B–E

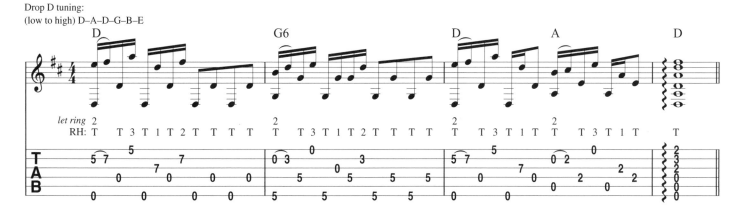

Now let's check out some Travis picking riffs that put Drop D tuning to use. Remember to let your thumb handle all the notes on strings 4, 5, and 6.

TRACK 48

DEAR PRUDENCE

Drop D Tuning:
(low to high) D–A–D–G–B–E

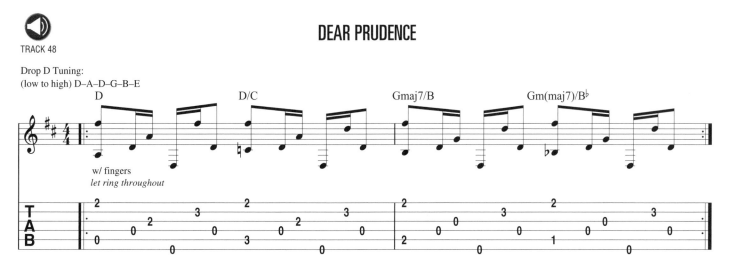

WATERSHED

Drop D tuning:
(low to high) D–A–D–G–B–E

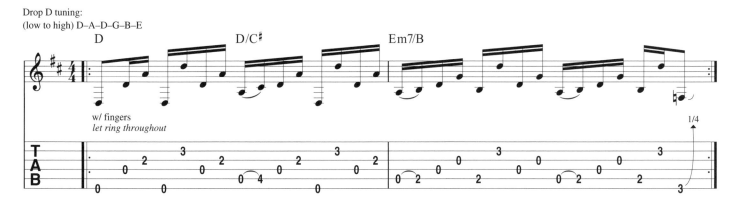

OTHER TUNINGS

Here are two more riffs from different tunings thrown in for good measure. Notice that the tunings differ only in the bottom two strings, so it shouldn't be too much trouble to try them both out. You'll need to lower your top two strings down a whole step for both of these riffs.

WHEN I WAS A BOY

Tuning:
(low to high) D–G–D–G–A–D

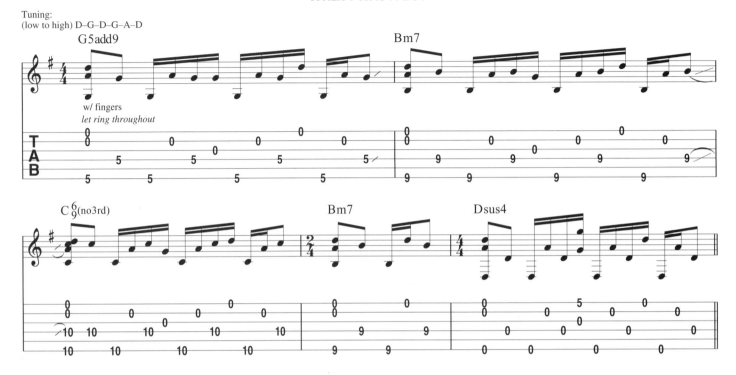

BUILDING A MYSTERY

TRACK 49

Capo VII

Tuning:
(low to high) E–A–D–G–A–D

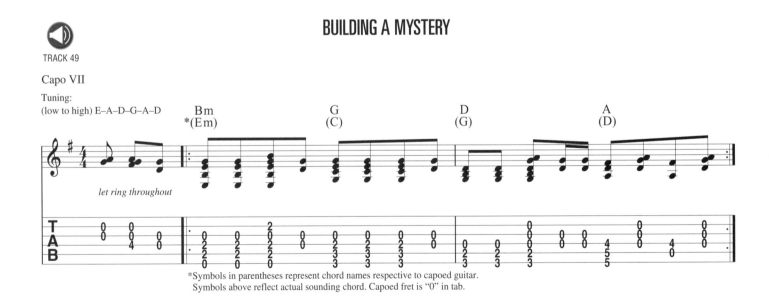

*Symbols in parentheses represent chord names respective to capoed guitar.
Symbols above reflect actual sounding chord. Capoed fret is "0" in tab.

Here is a list of some additional alternate tunings for you to explore. This is by no means comprehensive, but it's a good start. Feel free to add to this list by altering a string or two from one of these tunings. Experiment! Many times a tuning can inspire a whole song.

Double Drop D (D–A–D–G–B–D)

Dsus4 (D–A–D–G–A–D) (Often referred to as "Dadgad")

Open D (D–A–D–F♯–A–D)

Open Gm (D–G–D–G–B♭–D)

Open A (E–A–E–A–C♯–E)

Open E (E–B–E–G♯–B–E)

Open Em (E–B–E–G–B–E)

Open C (C–G–C–G–C–E)

JAM SESSION

Ok, assuming you haven't broken a string yet from all that retuning, it's time to jam out again. "Name" was the first in what would become a long string of hits for the Goo Goo Dolls in the late nineties. John Rzeznik makes use of a very unique tuning in this song—(low to high) D–A–E–A–E–E—to craft a beautiful acoustic guitar part. What's more, the main acoustic part is doubled by a second acoustic, creating a huge, lush sound. Regarding the tuning, in order to play the tune exactly as it sounds on the recording, you're going to need to replace your B string with another high E. However, you actually can approximate the sound by tuning your B string *down* to E. This won't sound exactly like the recording, but it still sounds great. Since the second string is not fretted throughout the entire song, the fact that it's loose and flappy doesn't cause much of an intonation problem. Now, you're welcome to try tuning your B string up to E, but I can't accept responsibility for what happens! You're likely to get stung in the face! If you have time, it's best to stick another high E string on there.

There are open strings ringing throughout this entire song. Your fret hand doesn't have too much action really, as many times only one finger is required. So just sit back and let this tuning work its magic!

NAME

TRACK 50

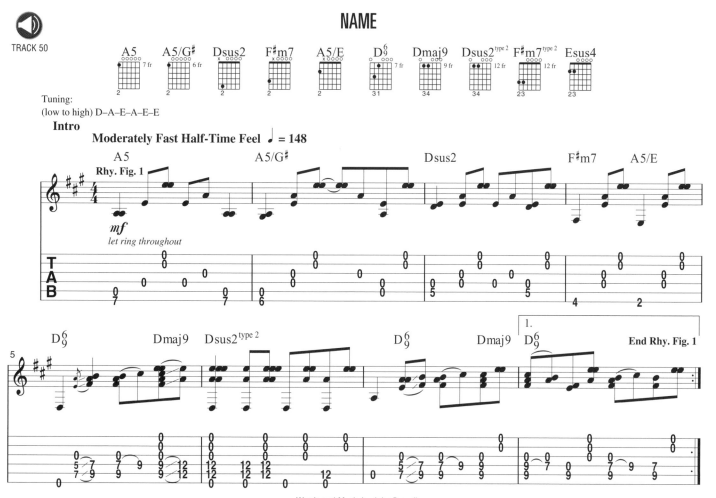

Words and Music by John Rzeznik

CHAPTER 5: COUNTRY & BLUEGRASS

Now we're going to take a look at some characteristic traits of country and bluegrass. While both of these styles can be considered "root" music and therefore share many qualities, there are some elements that are unique to each particular style. In this chapter, we'll examine the key elements and look at several riffs for each.

COUNTRY

The acoustic guitar has played a huge role in the history of country music, serving as a primary rhythm instrument, along with the piano, for countless hits. As country music continues to cross over into the pop and rock markets, electric guitars have enjoyed a growing usefulness, but it's highly unlikely that the acoustic will ever be exiled from the country world. The acoustic guitar's popularity has recently seen resurgence with the likes of the Dixie Chicks and Allison Kraus among others, assuring that its prognosis looks as good as ever.

The Ballad Strum

A commonly employed accompaniment technique in country music is the classic ballad strum pattern. This is a strumming style that involves alternating between a bass note on the low strings and a chord on the upper strings. The bass notes alternate usually between roots and 5ths. (We saw this a little earlier in the Travis picking section.) Performed by a solo acoustic, this technique provides a full-sounding accompaniment, nicely approximating the combined roles of the acoustic and bass in a full band setting.

TRACK 51

Here we see a slight variation on the above pattern.

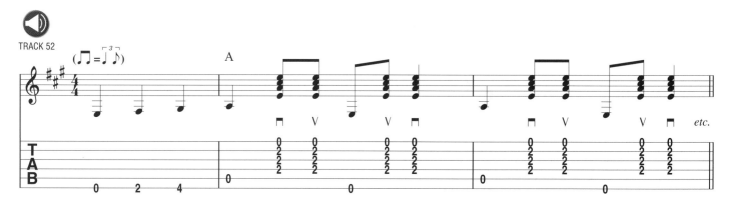

TRACK 52

44

This bass/strum approach can be adapted to a 3/4 waltz feel as well. This is a common feel for ballads.

TRACK 53

Now let's take a look at some classic examples of this approach.

BLUE MOON OF KENTUCKY

Words and Music by Bill Monroe
Copyright © 1947 by Peer International Corporation
Copyright Renewed
International Copyright Secured   All Rights Reserved

I'LL FLY AWAY

(sheet music notation for "I'LL FLY AWAY" with D, D7, G, D chords in standard notation and tablature)

BLUEGRASS

Though the line between bluegrass and country is often blurry, there are at least two characteristic traits of bluegrass that need mentioning. One of these is tempo. Bluegrass is often played at a brisk tempo and therefore requires a fairly high level of precision. If you've not yet mastered the art of playing in open position, you're going to get plenty of practice at it with bluegrass. The other is the flatpicking style. Whereas country music is almost an entirely vocal-dominated genre now, much bluegrass music still consists of guitars (and mandolins) flatpicking the melodies in an instrumental context. As mentioned, these tunes are often *fast* and will take some work getting up to speed.

Rhythm

From a rhythm guitar standpoint, the types of figures common in bluegrass are very similar to the bass-chord style we just learned in the country section. Hammer-on embellishments are quite common in bluegrass rhythm, as are walking bass runs. Let's take a look at a typical bluegrass rhythm pattern. Notice the common device of hammering from the 2nd degree of a chord to the 3rd on beat 3.

TRACK 54

46

"This Land is Your Land" by Woodie Guthrie contains some wonderful bluegrass rhythm playing.

THIS LAND IS YOUR LAND

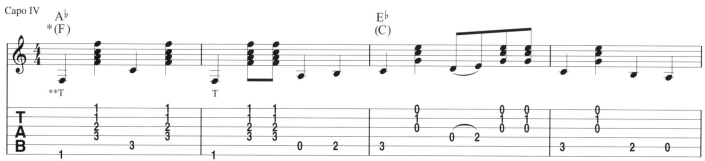

*Symbols in parentheses represent chord names respective to capoed guitar.
Symbols above reflect actual sounding chord. Capoed fret is "0" in tab.
**T = Thumb on 6th string

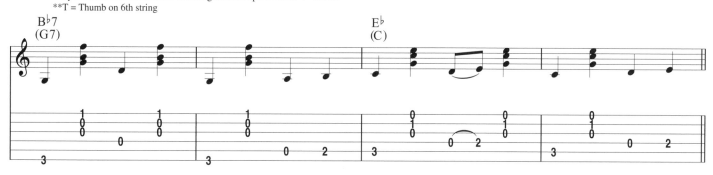

Flatpicking

If you're not quite sure what is meant by the term "flatpicking," don't worry. A flatpick is just your standard pick. The term originated to differentiate the between "flat" pick and the thumbpick, which was much more common in the earlier days of country and bluegrass. The term flatpicking now generally refers to the playing of brisk melodies in open position with a standard pick. That's not to say that flatpickers never stray from open position, but the melodies are often arranged there, as the tone of the open strings plays a big role in the desired sound.

Let's take a look at some major scale shapes arranged in open position in some of the most common flatpicking keys: C, G, and D.

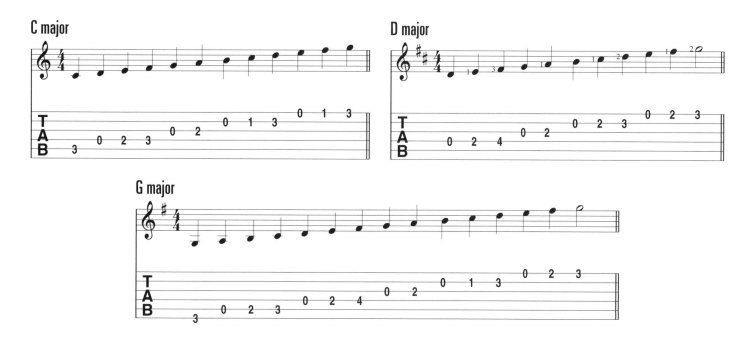

In order to play flatpicking tunes at the intended speed, you're going to need to be pretty comfortable with these scale shapes. Here are some exercises in each key to help get them under your fingers. Remember to use strict alternate picking on the eighth notes. Always pair downbeats with downstrokes and upbeats with upstrokes.

Now let's check out some flatpicking tunes. These will work great as solo tunes, or it will also sound great if you can find a friend to play the chords underneath. Remember to pair downbeats with downstrokes! To hear how this style should really sound, check out Doc Watson, Norman Blake, or Clarence White.

SOLDIER'S JOY

TRACK 55

BILLY IN THE LOW GROUND

TRACK 56

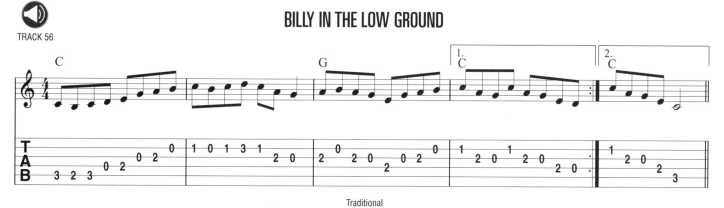

WHISKEY BEFORE BREAKFAST

TRACK 57

BLACKBERRY BLOSSOM

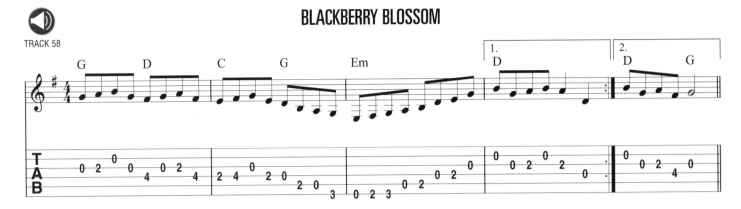

JAM SESSION

The Carter Family is undoubtedly one of the most influential bands in the history of country and bluegrass music. Along with perhaps Jimmie Rodgers, they were the first group to become superstars of the genre. A.P. Carter, the family patriarch, collected and arranged hundreds of British/Appalachian folk songs. With their more than 300 songs recorded, the Carter Family built the framework upon which the bluegrass style would stand for the next 50 years. The "Carter picking" style, as it would become known with their rise to popularity in the thirties, is evident here in "Wildwood Flower." The tempo here is quite brisk, so make sure you've got the bass/strum technique down well before diving in. Also, be sure to bring out the bass melody in the song's introduction.

WILDWOOD FLOWER

To Coda ⊕

1. Oh   I'll
2., 3., 4. *See additional lyrics*

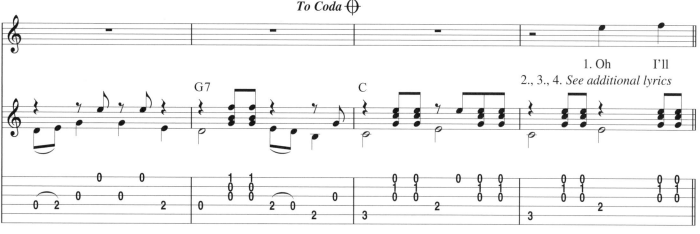

Verse

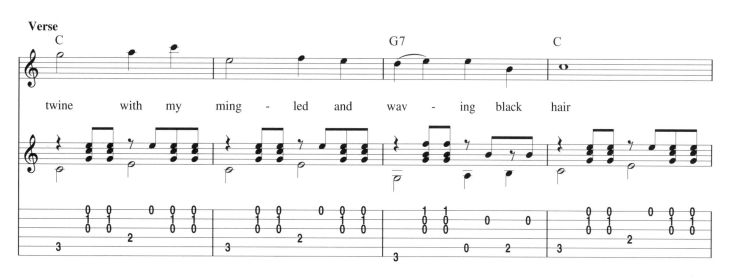

twine   with   my   ming - led   and   wav - ing   black   hair

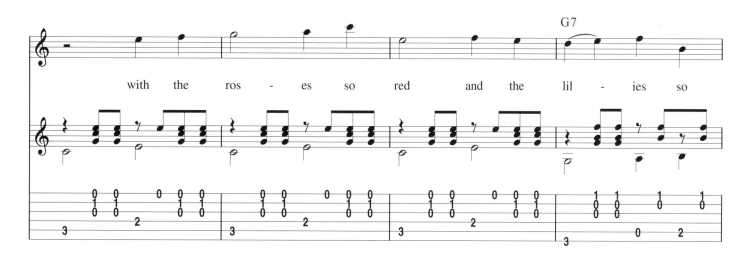

with   the   ros - es   so   red   and   the   lil - ies   so

Additional Lyrics

2. I will dance, I will sing and my life shall be gay.
   I will charm ev'ry heart, in his crown I will sway.
   When I woke from dreaming, my idols was clay.
   All portion of love had all flown away.

3. Oh, he taught me to love him and promised to love,
   And to cherish me over all others above.
   How my heart is now wond'ring, no misery can tell.
   He's left me no warning, no words of farewell.

4. Oh, he taught me to love him and called me his flower,
   That's blooming to cheer him through life's dreary hour.
   Oh, I long to see him and regret the dark hour.
   He's won and neglected this pale wildwood flower.

CHAPTER 6: BLUES SLIDE GUITAR

The blues genre is dominated nowadays, without question, by the guitar—specifically, the electric guitar. However, before Stevie Ray would wring the neck of his no. 1 Strat or B.B. would make Lucille yelp so gloriously, bluesmen like Son House, Skip James, and Robert Johnson had mastered the art of making their acoustic guitars cry for them. While string bending wasn't quite as practical on acoustic guitars, especially in those days, a slide was often employed to mimic the vocal quality of scooping into and "bending" notes.

Though the slide is used in standard tuning, it's much more frequently used in alternate tunings—especially in the blues. By far one of the most common is open G, as everything lays out better on the neck. So let's get into open G tuning and start playing some blues! If you can't remember how to get there, instructions can be found in the Alternate Tuning chapter. Note: Open A tuning is also frequently used, but since they are intervallically identical (e.g., open A is simply open G up a whole step), we'll just look at open G.

BLUES BASICS

Before we're able to play the blues, you'll need to have a basic understanding of the genre. If you're already familiar with the blues, skip on ahead. If not, this should get you up to speed.

Form

The blues is usually performed in what's called a "12-bar" form, consisting of the I, IV, and V chords. In the key of G, these would be G, C, and D. One of the defining traits that gives the blues its sound lies in the harmony; these three chords are usually all dominant seventh chords. Below we'll see a basic 12-bar blues in G. There are many variations on this form, but most don't stray too far from the example below.

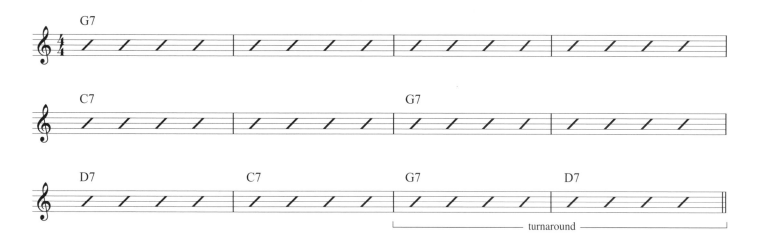

If you've spent any time learning music theory, you may have learned that the tonic chord (the I) is normally *not* a dominant 7th chord. Neither is the IV chord. The only chord that exists diatonically as a dominant seventh is the V chord. In fact, the term "dominant" refers to the 5th degree of a scale the same way "tonic" refers to the root (or first degree) of a scale. In blues, however, this is not the case. They are all dominant chords, yet they still function as they would in a diatonic setting.

Turnaround

The term "turnaround" refers to the last two bars of a blues progression, where it "turns around" back to the beginning. Again, there are many, many variations of the turnaround, and even more variations of turnaround licks. We're going to learn some of these in a bit.

Scales

Most of the licks or riffs heard in blues stem from one of four scales: the minor pentatonic, the blues scale, the major pentatonic, or the Mixolydian mode. This subject can get a little hairy, and it's beyond the scope of this book to cover it in depth, but we'll quickly look at the scales used on a chord-by-chord basis.

- Over the I chord (G7), the scales commonly used are G minor pentatonic (G–B♭–C–D–F), G blues (G–B♭–C–D♭–D–F), G major pentatonic (G–A–B–D–E), and G Mixolydian (G–A–B–C–D–E–F). Notice the blues scale only differs from the minor pentatonic by one note: the D♭, or ♭5th.

- The G minor pentatonic and G blues scales may also be used throughout the progression (over the I, IV, *and* V chords).

- Over the IV chord (C7), other scales commonly used are C major pentatonic (C–D–E–G–A) and C Mixolydian (C–D–E–F–G–A–B–C).

- Over the V chord (D7), other scales commonly used are D minor pentatonic (D–F–G–A–C), D major pentatonic (D–E–F♯–A–B), and D Mixolydian (D–E–F♯–G–A–B–C).

In practical application, these scales are commonly combined, and various positions on the neck may be covered. The upcoming examples in this chapter will demonstrate this. So now that you've got a basic understanding of the blues, let's get on with it.

SLIDE BASICS

There are many different types of slides available, but most fall into one of two categories: metal and glass. The tone will be slightly different, so you may want to buy one of each to see which one you prefer. You can usually find them for under $10.

The first thing you must decide is on which finger you'll wear the slide. The most popular seems to be the fourth finger, as this leaves the other three strongest fingers available for fretting. However, some people prefer their second finger, and occasionally you'll see people using their third finger. The next important issue concerning slide playing is tuning. In order to be in tune, you need to place the slide directly over the fret wire—not behind it as in normal fretting. Placing the slide behind the fret wire will cause you to be consistently flat. This may take a little getting used to at first, but very soon it will become second nature.

Let's try some simple slide riffs to get the technique down. These will be in the key of G.

TRACK 60

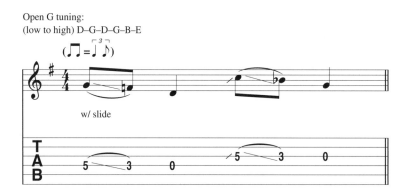

Ok, did you notice that things were kind of noisy during that last lick? Were you plucking the strings with a pick or your fingers? Most slide players prefer to use their fingers for plucking the strings because it makes something else much easier, *muting*. When playing slide, you're usually going to need to mute the strings that you aren't playing. Otherwise, the slide is going to make noise. Generally speaking, your palm will mute the lower strings, and your fingers will handle the higher strings. For instance, I use my right-hand first finger to pluck the first G note in the previous example. As I'm doing this, my palm is resting on string 6, my thumb is holding string 5, and fingers 2–4 are holding strings 3–1. If you start doing this properly in the beginning, eventually it too will become second nature.

Now let's try a few more melodies with the slide. Be sure you're in tune. You may want to record a G chord or have a friend play one underneath you so you can check your intonation.

TRACK 61

This lick makes use of vibrato on the last note. When performing vibrato with a slide, you're going to use a horizontal motion back and forth along the length of the string. Obviously, the farther you stray from the original position, the wider the vibrato.

TRACK 62

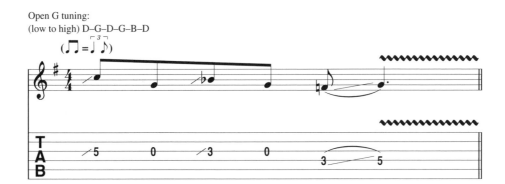

RHYTHM PATTERNS

Now we're going to look at some rhythm ideas for the I chord (G7). We'll begin with the most common blues rhythm of all: the boogie pattern. Notice how easy this pattern is in open G tuning. Regarding the right hand, try strumming both notes with the thumb or plucking the notes with the thumb and first finger. Alternatively, you can try a thumbpick and fingers.

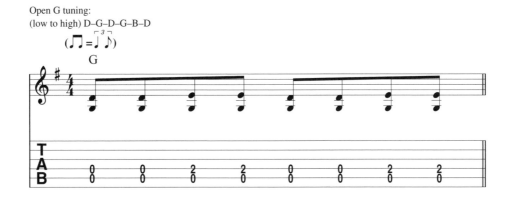

The boogie pattern is often simplified even more for a verse—rhythmically and/or harmonically. Below we'll see several examples of typical rhythm patterns you might run into. The ♭3rd (B♭, in this case) is used often in blues even over a major chord. This tension is largely responsible for the sound of the blues. Pay attention to the staccato marks—they're a big part of the sound. Notice that palm muting is sometimes applied to the bass notes; this aids in the separation between the bass and treble voices.

As we saw in Chapter 4, the open G tuning makes some unique voicings possible. Try strumming or fingerpicking the following chords in different combinations for one or two measures and see what you come up with. Maybe something like this:

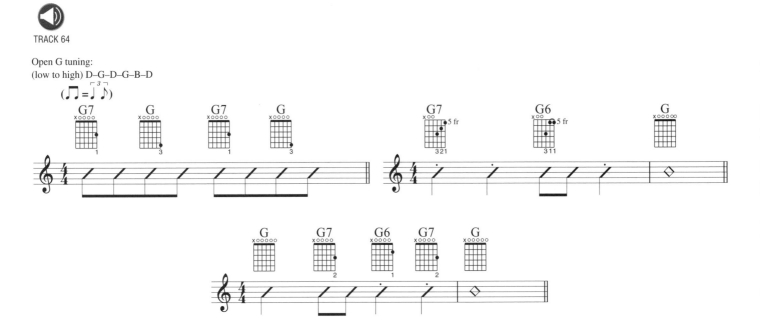

Though many times bluesmen will riff through the IV and V chords, similar voicings for the IV and V chords can be useful (see Chapter 4). You may have to stretch the third finger a bit; remember, you'll have a slide on your fourth finger.

Now that you've got some riffs, licks, and chords under your belt, let's see how the pros put them to use. Regarding the right hand here, I wish I could give some definitive directions, but really anything goes. Try strumming and plucking to see which one sounds best. One thing I can say is that you shouldn't use a standard pick if you want to be authentic. Use either a thumbpick or your bare fingers and peck out the notes however it sounds best! That's what they did.

MY BLACK MAMA

TRACK 65

Open G tuning:
(low to high) D–G–D–G–B–D

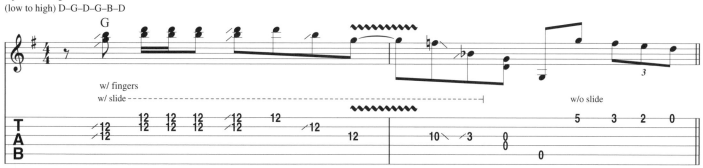

COME ON IN MY KITCHEN

TRACK 66

Open G tuning:
(low to high) D–G–D–G–B–D

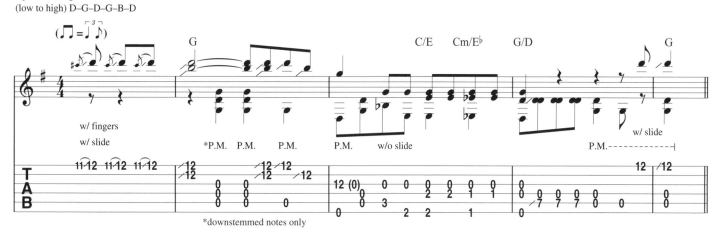

*downstemmed notes only

Open G tuning:
(low to high) D–G–D–G–B–D

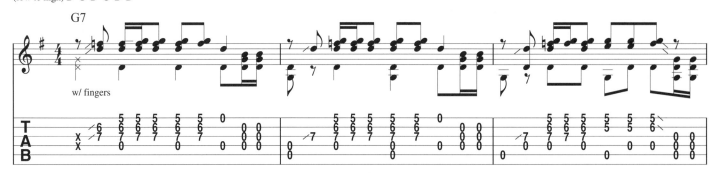

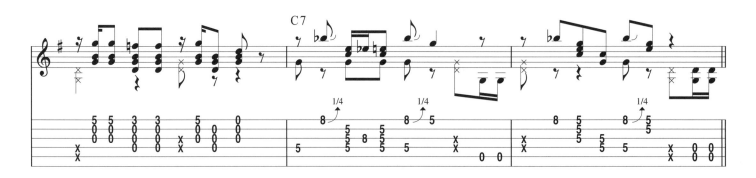

MY BLACK MAMA

Open G tuning:
(low to high) D–G–D–G–B–D

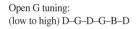

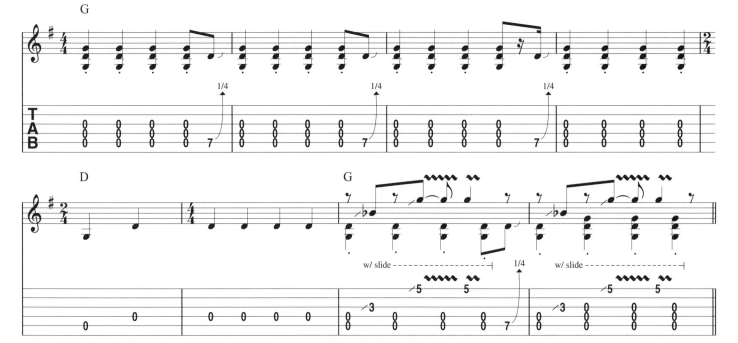

JAM SESSION

Who better to jam with than the "King of the Delta Blues" himself? Robert Johnson's contributions to the genre are incalculable, to say the least. "Cross Road Blues" stands as one of his most enduring classics, effectively demonstrating everything we've touched upon, and a bit more as well. (You may also recognize this song as it was famously covered by Eric Clapton with Cream in the sixties.)

One thing should be mentioned regarding form. Although we discussed the 12-bar blues form earlier, it's not going to appear intact in this song. Early bluesmen often extended parts to suit their need, resulting in uneven phrases and the occasional odd meter. The order of the chords, however, does resemble the 12-bar format. There will just be certain times when certain chords' durations will be augmented. Listen to the audio track if you have trouble with any of the phrasing or odd meters.

For other masters of the slide guitar, check out Son House or Booker White. To hear a current master's take on slide guitar, check out Bonnie Raitt. (Note: The following example was originally played in open G tuned up a half step with a capo on the second fret. It's presented here in open G with no capo for simplicity.)

TRACK 68

CROSS ROAD BLUES
(CROSSROADS)

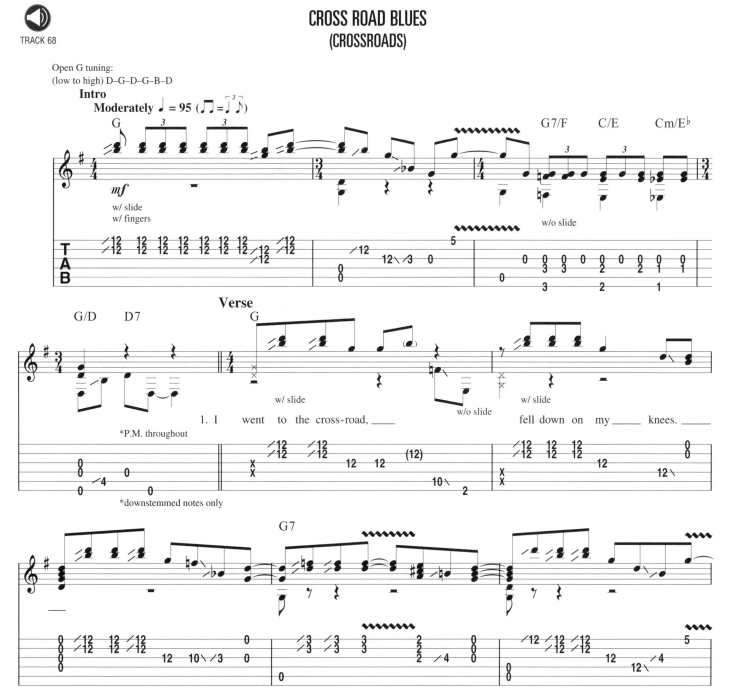

Words and Music by Robert Johnson
Copyright © (1978), 1990, 1991 Lehsem II, LLC and Claud L. Johnson
Administered by Music & Media International, Inc.
International Copyright Secured   All Rights Reserved

59

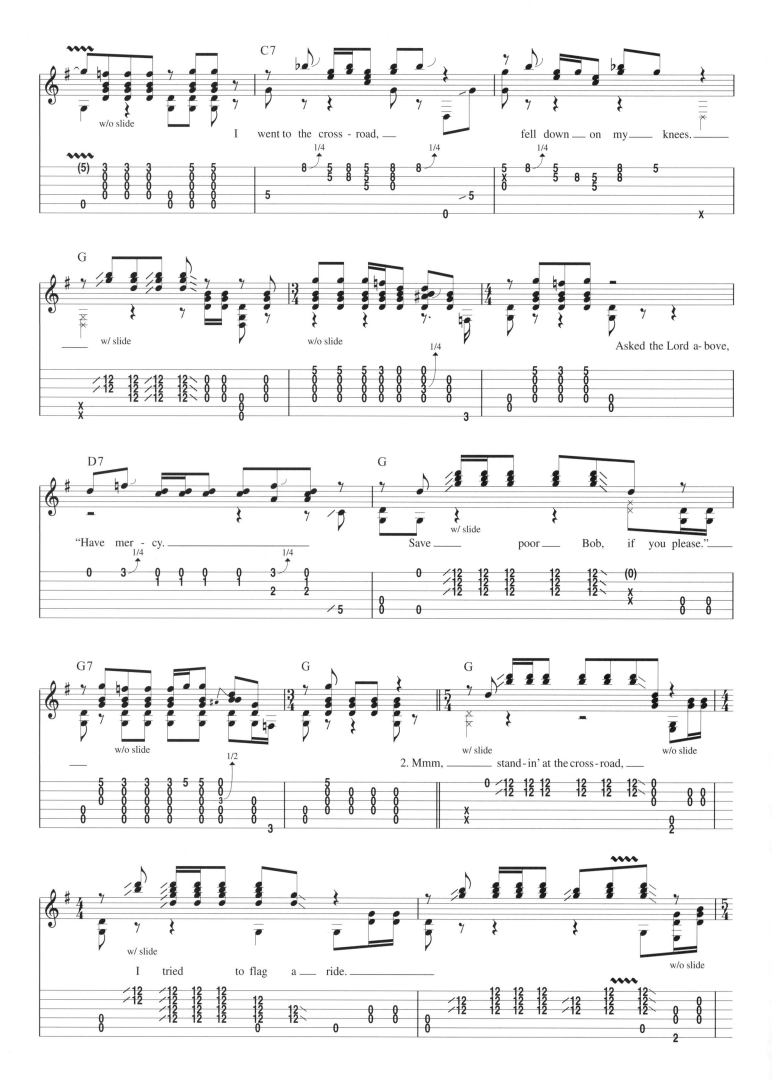

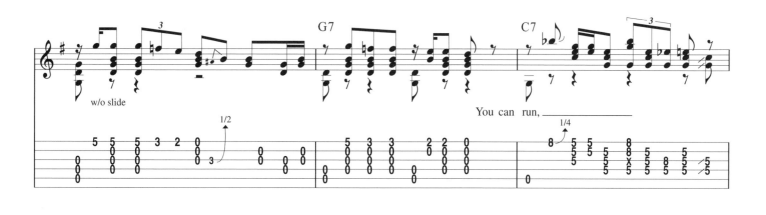

w/o slide

You can run, _____

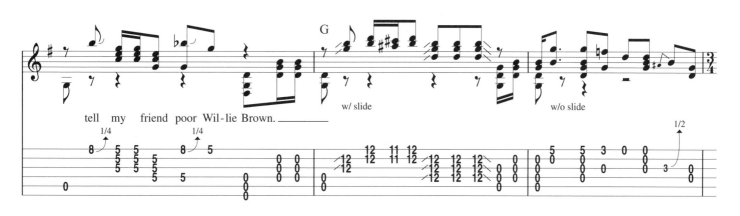

tell my friend poor Wil-lie Brown. _____

w/ slide   w/o slide

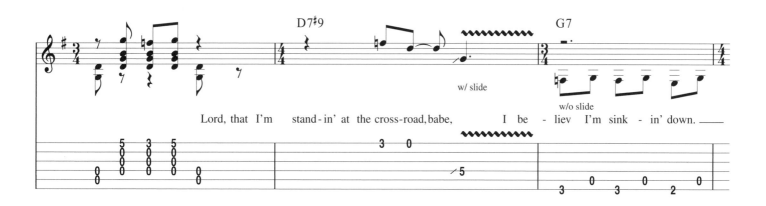

Lord, that I'm stand-in' at the cross-road, babe, I be - liev I'm sink - in' down. _____

w/ slide   w/o slide

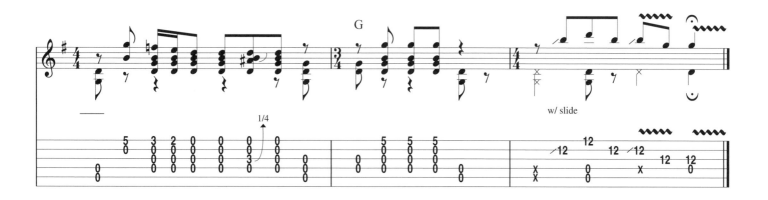

w/ slide

CHAPTER 7: ACOUSTIC RIFFS

While strumming and fingerpicking patterns certainly account for a large percentage of acoustic playing, let's not forget about riffs. Players of all genres have exploited the instrument's inimitable timbre to create some lasting gems. In this chapter, we're going to take a look at some riff concepts that often find their way into the realm of acoustic guitar.

DRONING STRINGS

There's nothing quite like the tone of open strings on an acoustic guitar. While barre chords still sound great in their own way, an acoustic guitar really gets to strut its stuff when some open strings are allowed to ring out. Here we're going to take a look at riffs that make open strings, both low and high, an integral part of their sound.

Let's start out with a simple exercise to help illustrate the concept a bit. An easy way to get your feet wet with drones is to simply take an open-position chord and move the fret-hand shape up to the respective IV and V chords of that key while allowing the open strings to continue to ring. If we were in D for example, the I chord would be D, the IV chord would be G, and the V would be A. Here's what this would look like:

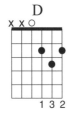
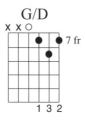
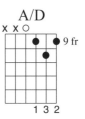

If we try the same thing in C, the chord shapes would be C, F, and G. Check out the interesting harmonies created here with the open E and G strings ringing.

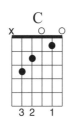
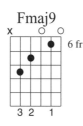
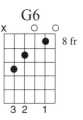

Here's the same idea in the key of E. The shapes are built off the E, A, and B chords, but the resulting harmonies are much more interesting than the typical I–IV–V variety.

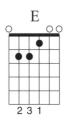
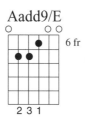
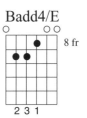

Now if we apply some of the different technical treatments we've learned thus far (strumming, Travis picking, arpeggiation) to these chords, we end up with some unique riffs. Maybe something like these:

This type of approach can be used with all the diatonic chords of a key—not just the I, IV, and V. Here we'll move up diatonically through the keys of D, A, and E. Pay special attention to the colorful harmonies that are created by the open-string drones.

Key of D

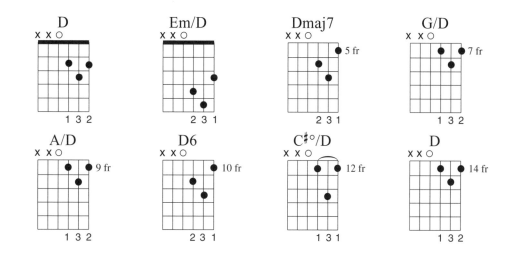

Key of A

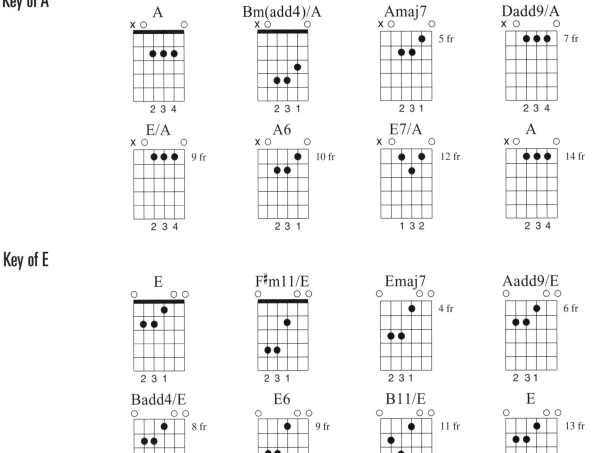

Key of E

By including an expressive device, such as slides, things can get even more interesting. Try the examples below to hear this approach.

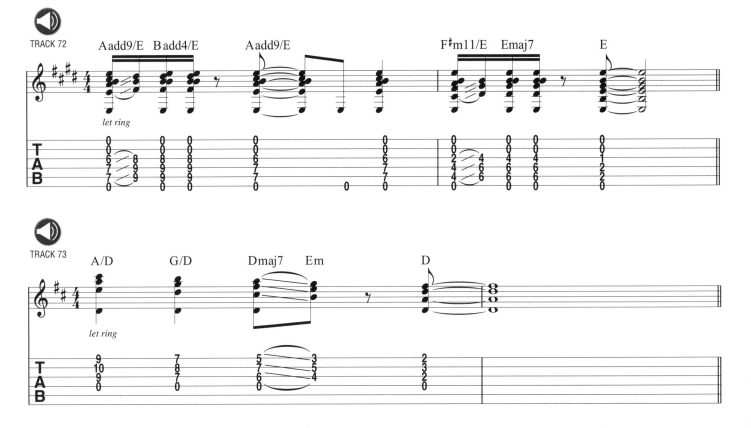

Even something as simple as a power chord can sound fresh when combined with droning strings.

Here are some examples of droning strings at work in some classic riffs.

CLOSER TO FINE

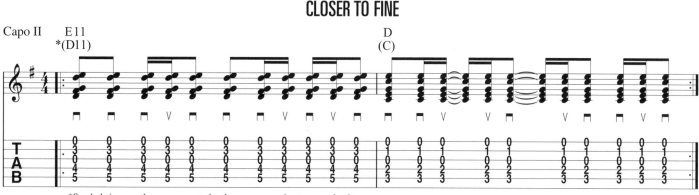

*Symbols in parentheses represent chord names respective to capoed guitar.
Symbols above reflect actual sounding chord. Capoed fret is "0" in tab.

DUST IN THE WIND

HEAVEN BESIDE YOU

CHORDAL EMBELLISHMENTS

This technique involves the brief dressing up of a chord with a neighboring note (or two), adding elements of harmonic and rhythmic interest. The suspended 4th is one of the most common examples of this device, but as we'll see here, there are many other possibilities.

Let's take a look at a simple example. Here we're embellishing a simple D chord with a G note and the open E string. The harmonies that are created are Dsus4 and Dsus2. The name stems from the fact the 3rd of the chord (F♯) is being "suspended" temporarily.

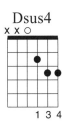
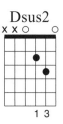

Here's the same device transposed to several different chords. Notice the subtle adjustments that need to be made for each chord shape (e.g., avoiding the open high E string on the Csus2 chord, which would be a 3rd). For some chords, such as E, there's not a practical way to suspend the 2nd. The 4th, however, is often suspended as shown.

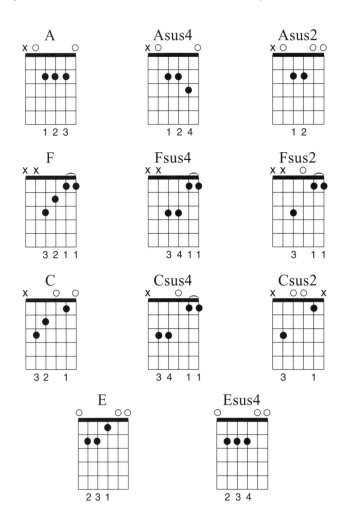

Other common embellishments include the 6th and the 9th. Here we'll see several examples of these. (Note: The 9th is actually the same note as the 2nd. The way you decide on how to name the chord depends on the presence of the 3rd. If the 3rd is present, the note is called a 9th. If the third is not present, then you've usually got a sus2 chord.)

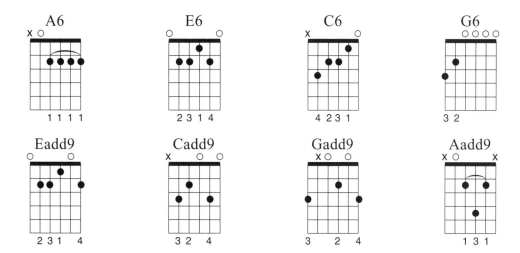

Occasionally, the major 7th is used as an embellishment.

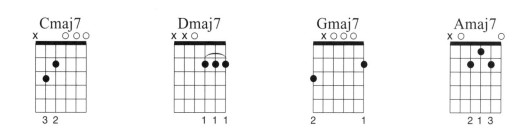

Regarding the playing of these embellishments, there are a few different technical possibilities. Simply strumming through them is probably the most common method. Here are some examples of this method.

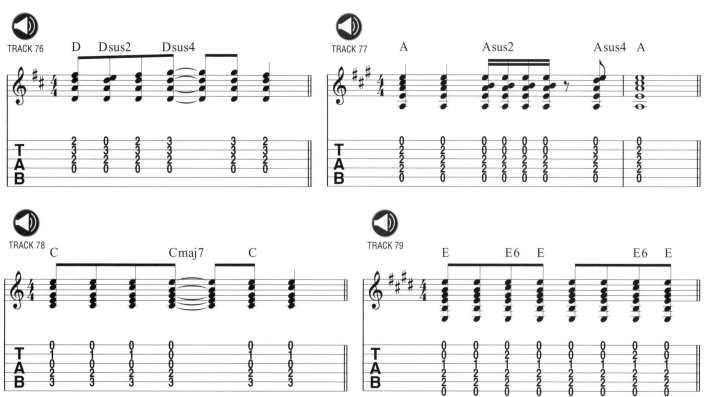

Hammering on or pulling off to these embellishments is another possibility. Check out the examples below to see how this works.

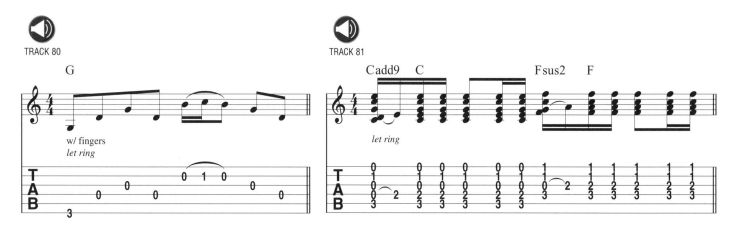

Now let's take a look at some of these embellishments in some real riffs.

BEHIND BLUE EYES

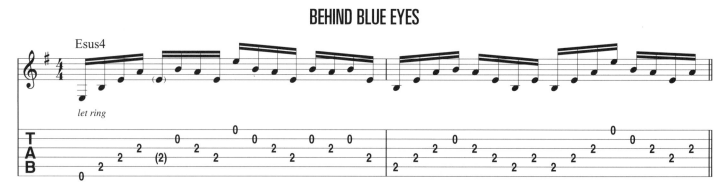

JACK AND DIANE

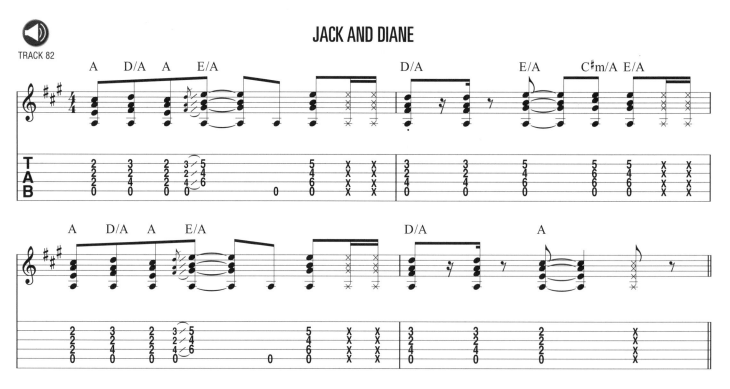

CHANGE THE WORLD

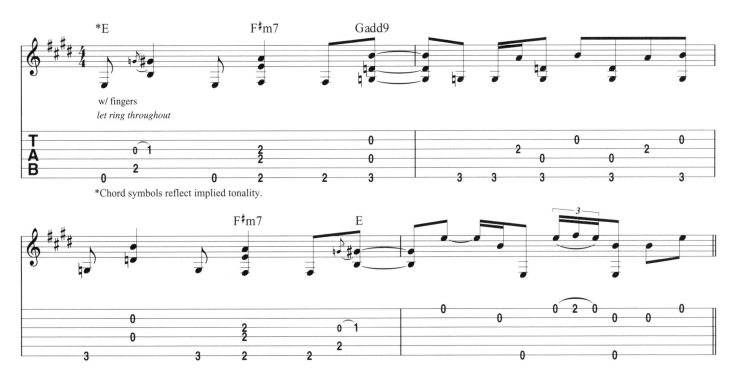

Words and Music by Wayne Kirkpatrick, Gordon Kennedy and Tommy Sims
Copyright © 1996 by Careers-BMG Music Publishing, Inc., Magic Beans Music, BMG Songs, Inc.,
Universal - PolyGram International Publishing, Inc. and Universal - MCA Music Publishing
International Copyright Secured   All Rights Reserved

FREE FALLIN'

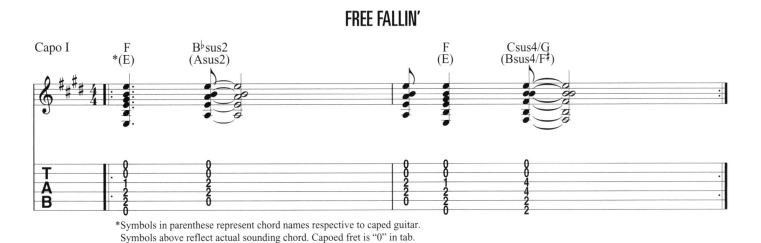

*Symbols in parenthese represent chord names respective to caped guitar.
Symbols above reflect actual sounding chord. Capoed fret is "0" in tab.

Words and Music by Tom Petty and Jeff Lynne
© 1989 EMI APRIL MUSIC INC. and GONE GATOR MUSIC
All Rights Reserved   International Copyright Secured   Used by Permission

JAM SESSION

OK, it's time to jam along with "the greatest rock 'n' roll band in the world." The Rolling Stones' Keith Richards, considered by some the greatest rhythm riff guitarist of all time, puts his acoustic up front in support of their classic "Angie." Combining arpeggiation and strumming, Keith creates a both interesting and supportive rhythm guitar part.

The instrumentation is augmented in the first chorus with the entrance of a 12-string acoustic strumming along (arranged here for 6-string). Richards places numerous rhythmic gems throughout the song, demonstrated perfectly in measures 17–18, where he answers the song's main A minor pentatonic hook with a chromatic neighboring riff over E7. Be sure to notice how Richards includes numerous chordal embellishments, always maintaining the attention of the listener.

ANGIE

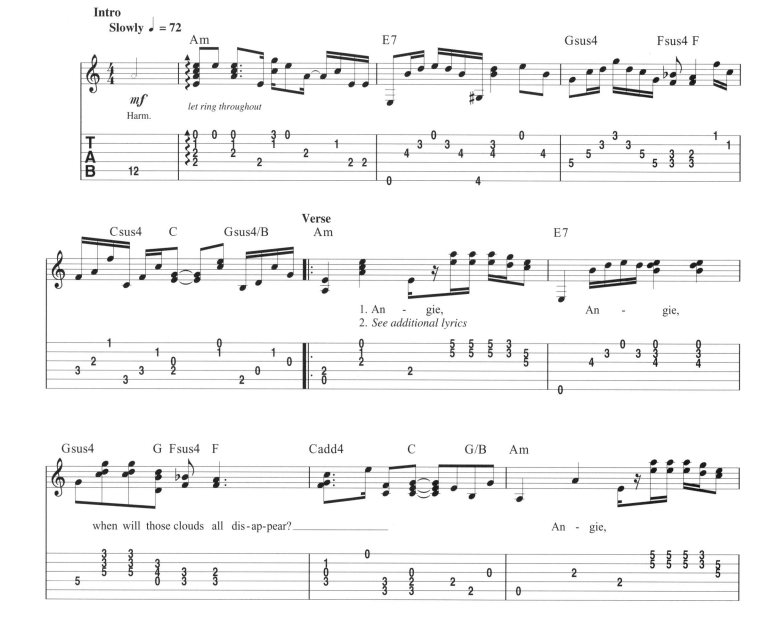

Words and Music by Mick Jagger and Keith Richards
© 1973 (Renewed 2001) EMI MUSIC PUBLISHING LTD.
All Rights for the U.S. and Canada Controlled and Administered by COLGEMS-EMI MUSIC INC.
All Rights Reserved   International Copyright Secured   Used by Permission

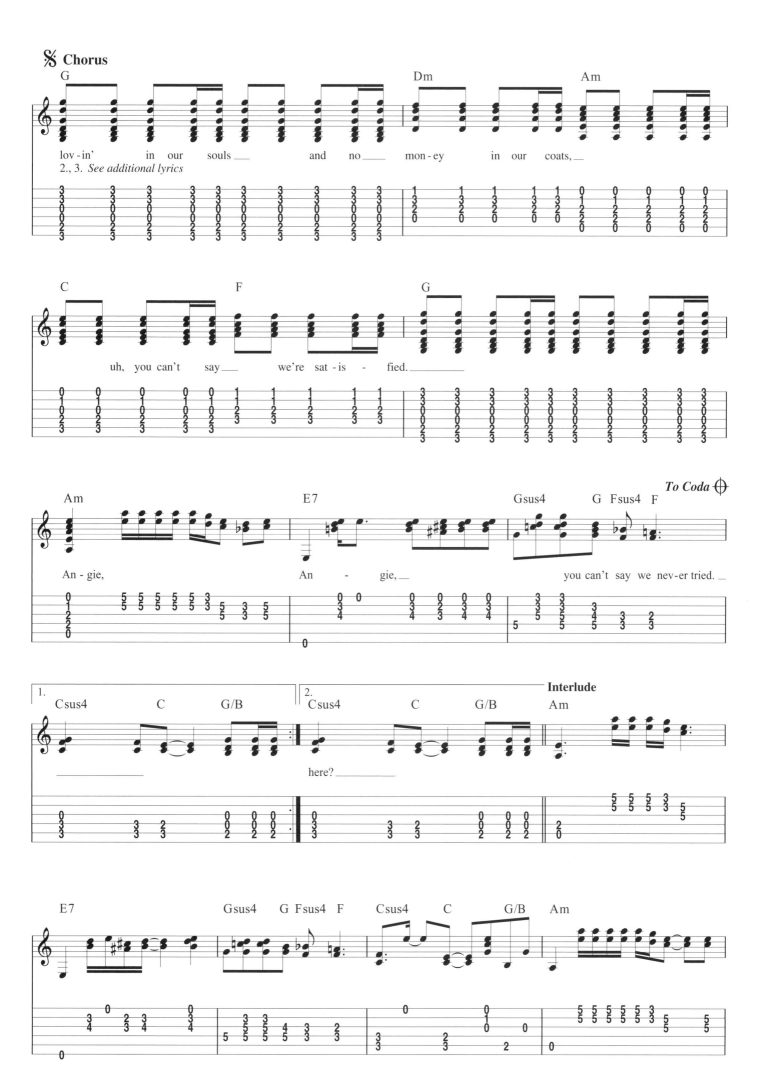

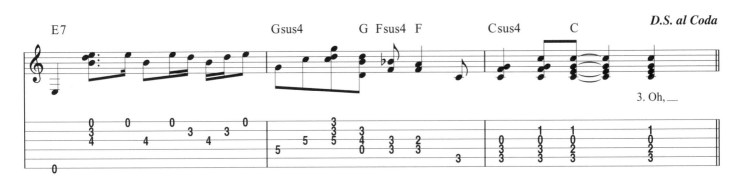

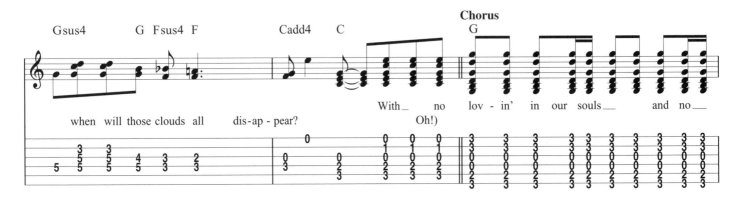

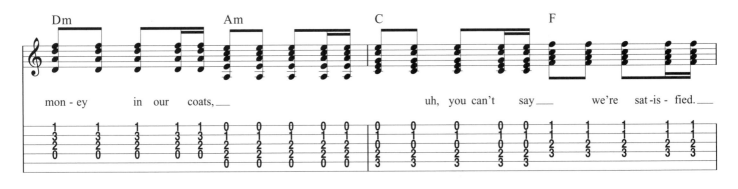

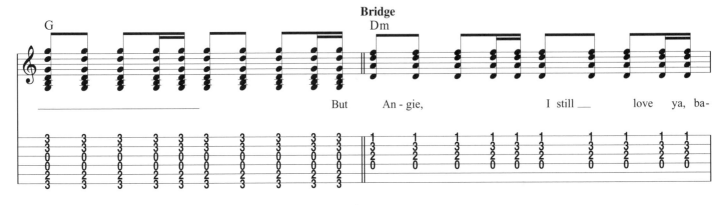

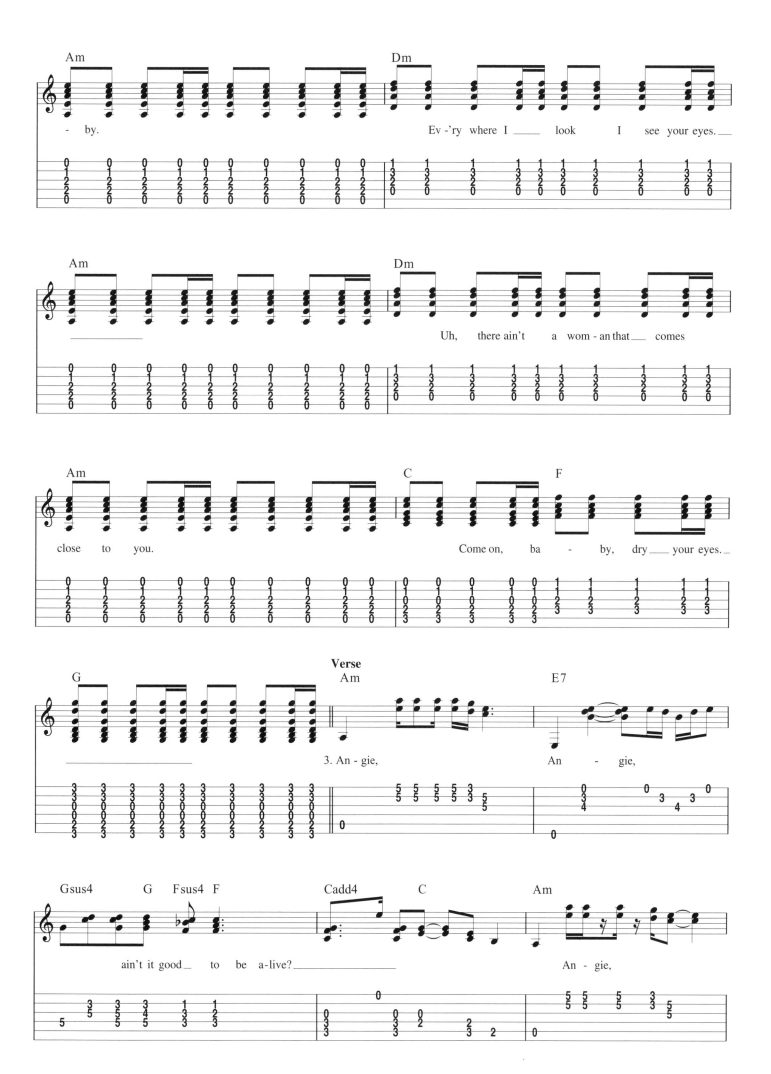

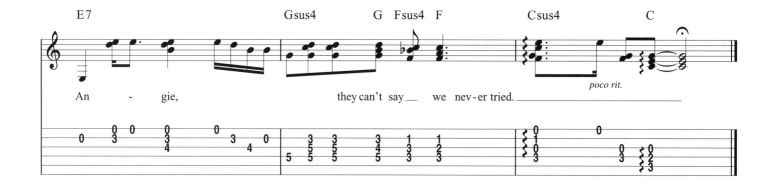

An - gie,   they can't say __ we nev-er tried. _____

Additional Lyrics

2. A-Angie, you're beautiful, yes,
   But ain't it time we said good-bye?
   A-Angie, I still love ya.
   Remember all those nights we cried?

Chorus 2. All the dreams we held so close
   Seemed to all go up in smoke.
   Uh, let me whisper in your ear.
   Whispered: Angie, Angie,
   Where will it lead us from here?

Chorus 3. Oh, Angie, don't you weep,
   All your kisses still taste sweet.
   I hate that sadness in your eyes.
   But Angie, Angie,
   A-Ain't it time we said good-bye?

AFTERWORD

Well, that does it for the Hal Leonard Acoustic Guitar method. Hopefully you've gained a good grasp on several usable acoustic guitar techniques and an understanding of when and how to apply them. Don't be afraid to incorporate elements of these players into your style. This is how new styles are born. Remember that there's always something new to learn, and keep an open mind. Have fun!

Guitar Notation Legend

Guitar Music can be notated three different ways: on a *musical staff*, in *tablature*, and in *rhythm slashes*.

RHYTHM SLASHES are written above the staff. Strum chords in the rhythm indicated. Use the chord diagrams found at the top of the first page of the transcription for the appropriate chord voicings. Round noteheads indicate single notes.

THE MUSICAL STAFF shows pitches and rhythms and is divided by bar lines into measures. Pitches are named after the first seven letters of the alphabet.

TABLATURE graphically represents the guitar fingerboard. Each horizontal line represents a a string, and each number represents a fret.

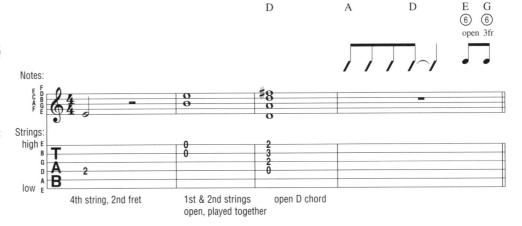

4th string, 2nd fret — 1st & 2nd strings open, played together — open D chord

Definitions for Special Guitar Notation

HALF-STEP BEND: Strike the note and bend up 1/2 step.

WHOLE-STEP BEND: Strike the note and bend up one step.

GRACE NOTE BEND: Strike the note and immediately bend up as indicated.

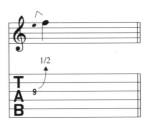

SLIGHT (MICROTONE) BEND: Strike the note and bend up 1/4 step.

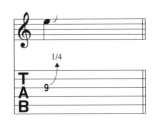

BEND AND RELEASE: Strike the note and bend up as indicated, then release back to the original note. Only the first note is struck.

PRE-BEND: Bend the note as indicated, then strike it.

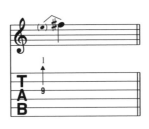

PRE-BEND AND RELEASE: Bend the note as indicated. Strike it and release the bend back to the original note.

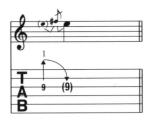

UNISON BEND: Strike the two notes simultaneously and bend the lower note up to the pitch of the higher.

VIBRATO: The string is vibrated by rapidly bending and releasing the note with the fretting hand.

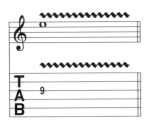

WIDE VIBRATO: The pitch is varied to a greater degree by vibrating with the fretting hand.

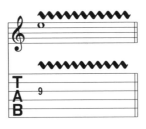

HAMMER-ON: Strike the first (lower) note with one finger, then sound the higher note (on the same string) with another finger by fretting it without picking.

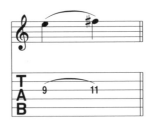

PULL-OFF: Place both fingers on the notes to be sounded. Strike the first note and without picking, pull the finger off to sound the second (lower) note.

LEGATO SLIDE: Strike the first note and then slide the same fret-hand finger up or down to the second note. The second note is not struck.

SHIFT SLIDE: Same as legato slide, except the second note is struck.

TRILL: Very rapidly alternate between the notes indicated by continuously hammering on and pulling off.

TAPPING: Hammer ("tap") the fret indicated with the pick-hand index or middle finger and pull off to the note fretted by the fret hand.

NATURAL HARMONIC: Strike the note while the fret-hand lightly touches the string directly over the fret indicated.

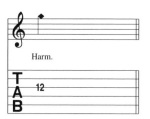

PINCH HARMONIC: The note is fretted normally and a harmonic is produced by adding the edge of the thumb or the tip of the index finger of the pick hand to the normal pick attack.

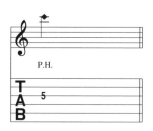

HARP HARMONIC: The note is fretted normally and a harmonic is produced by gently resting the pick hand's index finger directly above the indicated fret (in parentheses) while the pick hand's thumb or pick assists by plucking the appropriate string.

PICK SCRAPE: The edge of the pick is rubbed down (or up) the string, producing a scratchy sound.

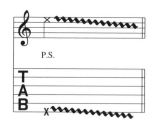

MUFFLED STRINGS: A percussive sound is produced by laying the fret hand across the string(s) without depressing, and striking them with the pick hand.

PALM MUTING: The note is partially muted by the pick hand lightly touching the string(s) just before the bridge.

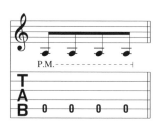

RAKE: Drag the pick across the strings indicated with a single motion.

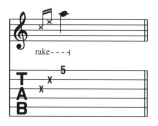

TREMOLO PICKING: The note is picked as rapidly and continuously as possible.

ARPEGGIATE: Play the notes of the chord indicated by quickly rolling them from bottom to top.

VIBRATO BAR DIVE AND RETURN: The pitch of the note or chord is dropped a specified number of steps (in rhythm) then returned to the original pitch.

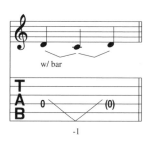

VIBRATO BAR SCOOP: Depress the bar just before striking the note, then quickly release the bar.

VIBRATO BAR DIP: Strike the note and then immediately drop a specified number of steps, then release back to the original pitch.

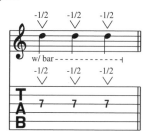

Additional Musical Definitions

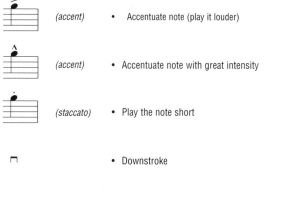

(accent)	•	Accentuate note (play it louder)
(accent)	•	Accentuate note with great intensity
(staccato)	•	Play the note short
⊓	•	Downstroke
∨	•	Upstroke

D.S. al Coda • Go back to the sign (𝄋), then play until the measure marked "*To Coda*," then skip to the section labelled "**Coda**."

D.C. al Fine • Go back to the beginning of the song and play until the measure marked "*Fine*" (end).

Rhy. Fig. • Label used to recall a recurring accompaniment pattern (usually chordal).

Riff • Label used to recall composed, melodic lines (usually single notes) which recur.

Fill • Label used to identify a brief melodic figure which is to be inserted into the arrangement.

Rhy. Fill • A chordal version of a Fill.

tacet • Instrument is silent (drops out).

• Repeat measures between signs.

1. 2. • When a repeated section has different endings, play the first ending only the first time and the second ending only the second time.

NOTE: Tablature numbers in parentheses mean:
1. The note is being sustained over a system (note in standard notation is tied), or
2. The note is sustained, but a new articulation (such as a hammer-on, pull-off, slide or vibrato begins), or
3. The note is a barely audible "ghost" note (note in standard notation is also in parentheses).

HAL LEONARD GUITAR METHOD BOOK 1
SECOND EDITION
CD INCLUDED
BY WILL SCHMID AND GREG KOCH

HAL LEONARD GUITAR METHOD

THE HAL LEONARD GUITAR METHOD is designed for anyone just learning to play acoustic or electric guitar. It is based on years of teaching guitar students of all ages, and it also reflects some of the best guitar teaching ideas from around the world. This comprehensive method includes: Learning sequence carefully paced with clear instructions; popular songs which increase the incentive to learn to play; versatility – can be used as self-instruction or with a teacher; audio accompaniments so that students have fun and sound great while practicing.

BOOK 1
Book 1 provides beginning instruction which includes tuning, playing position, musical symbols, notes in first position, the C, G, G7, D, D7, A7, and Em chords, rhythms through eighth notes, strumming and picking, 100 great songs, riffs, and examples. Includes a chord chart and well-known songs: Ode to Joy • Rockin' Robin • Greensleeves • Give My Regards to Broadway • Time Is on My Side.
00699010 Book $5.95
00699027 Book/CD Pack $9.95

BOOK 2
Book 2 continues the instruction started in Book 1 and covers: Am, Dm, A, E, F and B7 chords; power chords; finger-style guitar; syncopations, dotted rhythms, and triplets; Carter style solos; bass runs; pentatonic scales; improvising; tablature; 92 great songs, riffs and examples; notes in first and second position; and more! The CD includes 57 full-band tracks.
00699020 Book $5.95
00697313 Book/CD Pack $9.95

BOOK 3
Book 3 covers: the major, minor, pentatonic, and chromatic scales, sixteenth notes; barre chords; drop D tuning; movable scales; notes in fifth position; slides, hammer-ons, pull-offs, and string bends; chord construction; gear; 90 great songs, riffs, and examples; and more! The CD includes 61 full-band tracks.
00699030 Book $5.95
00697316 Book/CD Pack $9.95

COMPOSITE
Books 1, 2, and 3 bound together in an easy-to-use spiral binding.
00699040 Books Only $14.95
00697342 Book/3-CD Pack $22.95

VIDEO AND DVD
FOR THE BEGINNING ELECTRIC OR ACOUSTIC GUITARIST
00697318 DVD $19.95
00320159 VHS Video $14.95
00697341 Book/CD Pack and DVD $24.95

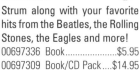